DRIVING

POWER & PRECISION

GAME IMPROVEMENT LIBRARY™

CREDITS

DRIVING
Power & Precision

Printed in 2004.

Tom Carpenter
Creative Director

Julie Cisler
Senior Book Design & Production

Jen Weaverling
Senior Book Development Coordinator

Steve Hosid
Instruction Editor/Photographer

Steve Ellis
Editor

Ward Clayton
Leo McCullagh
John Morris
Mike Mueller
PGA TOUR

Bruce Holt
Proofreader

Special thanks to the following Golf Clubs for allowing us to shoot on location
TPC of Scottsdale
Wood Ranch
La Quinta
Rancho Cordova
Arnold Palmer's Bay Hill Club

Acknowledgements
"To the members of the PGA TOUR Partners Club I meet at Tournaments around the Country: Your questions, comments and support help create articles and books that truly reflect the needs of our outstanding membership." —*Steve Hosid*

3 4 5 6 7 8 / 07 06 05 04
ISBN 1-58159-114-4
© 2000 PGA TOUR Partners Club

PGA TOUR Partners Club
12301 Whitewater Drive
Minnetonka, Minnesota 55343

Visit the PGA TOUR Partners Club Web Site at:
www.partnersclubonline.com

ABOUT THE AUTHOR/ PHOTOGRAPHER

Steve Hosid is instruction editor, contributing writer and photographer for *PGA TOUR Partners* magazine. He is coauthor of *The Complete Idiot's Guide to Healthy Stretching* (with Chris Verna), and *Golf for Everybody* (with Brad Brewer, director of The Arnold Palmer Golf Academies). He has also collaborated on books with LPGA star Michelle McGann and tennis player MaliVai Washington.

Steve is a graduate of the University of Southern California and has produced and hosted several television and radio shows in Los Angeles. These days his appearances revolve around golf on the PGA TOUR.

He lives with his wife, Jill, and two non-golfing Borzoi Wolfhounds on the 13th hole at Arnold Palmer's Bay Hill Club in Orlando, Florida.

Author/photographer Steve Hosid (left) with his friend Arnold Palmer.

TABLE OF CONTENTS

INTRODUCTION

As *PGA TOUR Partners* magazine instruction editor, I get to spend PGA TOUR tournaments at my favorite place—the practice range. Watching the game's greatest players is always an inspiration. This book is your pass to join me for a firsthand look at how four outstanding TOUR professionals drive for power (distance) and precision (accuracy).

In *Driving—Power & Precision*, these professionals take an active interest in helping you—their fellow PGA TOUR Partners Club member—become a better, more accurate driver. They speak directly to you, sharing their thoughts and suggestions.

John Daly and John Jacobs consistently rank at or near the top of their respective TOURs in driving distance. Scott McCarron, who stands 5-foot-10 and weighs 165 pounds, drives the ball over 290 yards. Steve Pate is not the longest player off the tee, but after years of injuries has formed solid swing fundamentals that have helped him regain status as one of the TOUR's top players.

I've known all four players for years, and I know they have an active interest in helping you. I watch them help other golfers every week—their amateur partners in pro-ams.

These pros will help you analyze your game off the tee. Then it's off to the course for a close-up look at each phase of *their* swings. They also offer advice on correcting common problems, help you select the right equipment, and demonstrate principles for increasing clubhead speed.

In addition, nationally-known golf instructor Martin Hall, whose Partners Club video appearances have helped many members, will help you better understand the advice of our professionals with his "Practice Tee" sections located throughout the book.

You also will learn how former British Open and two-time PGA champion Nick Price prepares for a round, as he stretches with rotational specialist Chris "Mr. Stretch" Verna.

Finally, our four TOUR players conclude the book by sharing inside information on TOUR techniques that will make your drives longer and more accurate.

You are about to get outstanding instruction from your fellow members, straight from the TOUR, so join me as we start you on the road to driving with more power and precision.

-Steve Hosid-

MEET THE PLAYERS

JOHN DALY

Birth Date: April 28, 1966

Height: 5'11"

Weight: 220

College: University of Arkansas

Driving: 305.6 yards average.

Winner 1991 PGA Championship, 1995 British Open

JOHN JACOBS

Birth Date: March 18, 1945

Height: 6'3"

Weight: 225

College: University of Southern California

Driving: 285.7 yards average.

I have a tough time when my game is off, but it's my living. As an amateur golfer your only goal should be to have fun when you play, and never look at it as work. If you hit a bad shot—and you will—don't worry about it.

Sometimes golf can be frustrating for all golfers. A few years ago during the Bay Hill Invitational, I had a really bad hole and ended up with an 18.

Bay Hill's 6th hole is a 543-yard par-5 that wraps around a lake. I wasn't aiming across the water at the green, but I had a severe case of the "duck hooks." The farther I aimed to the right and away from the water, the more I hooked it into the water. It got to the point where it was funny and the fans started yelling "Tin Cup, Tin Cup," so I kept hitting my driver instead of an iron.

I was down to my last ball. Fortunately, when the ball hooked back toward the water it hit the rocks and bounced back into play. I made it to the green in 16, facing a 30-footer for a 17. I lipped out for an 18. I didn't let this get to me. Instead of getting angry, I realized the crowd was entertained. I birdied the next hole. Golf is a game, so enjoy it.

—John Daly

D riving distance is compatible with driving accuracy. On the two holes our distance is measured at SENIOR PGA TOUR tournaments, the ball often will roll into the first cut of rough by a couple of yards. While my accuracy ranking was average, I probably missed 60 percent of the fairways by only three or four yards.

If accuracy was the prime consideration, those of us who are long would gear back and hit it straighter. The problem is that when we try to hit it too far, we lose accuracy.

How many times do you think I hit my driver during a round? I pull my driver six to nine times, and only when the hole requires extra length. The rest of the time I hit irons or fairway woods.

Driving is not something I need to practice a lot because it comes naturally to me. My slumps are caused by a lack of accuracy, and are fixed by checking my alignment and weight transfer. For every hour I practice driving, I spend 10 hours practicing chipping.

—John Jacobs

Scott McCarron

Birth Date: July 10, 1965
Height: 5'10"
Weight: 165
College: UCLA
Driving: 287.1 yards average.

One of the keys to becoming a good driver is relaxation. Being nervous causes you to get quick, and that's how trouble starts. Swinging fast is not the same as swinging hard. Pros make the same mistake. When I start getting a little quick, it's usually at the top of my backswing.

During pro-ams my amateur partners run the gamut of emotions. They may start off nervous and play poorly, then they hit a good drive and suddenly they've "found the secret" and are ready to take on Arnold Palmer. This is usually followed by more inconsistency as they begin changing everything.

Professionals, on the other hand, never work on their games during a round. The reality is that we are going to hit a bad shot occasionally, but that doesn't mean the entire swing needs to be revamped during the round. Any changes are made later on the practice tee. During the round we stay focused on getting the ball into the hole.

There was a time when I actually gave up competitive golf. For four years I worked with my dad in his clothing business. As a spectator during the SENIOR PGA TOUR's 1991 Raley's Gold Rush Classic, my desire to play competitive golf was rekindled. I went home, built a long-handled putter in the garage and nearly won the U. S. Mid-Amateur that year. Three years later I earned my PGA TOUR playing card.

—Scott McCarron

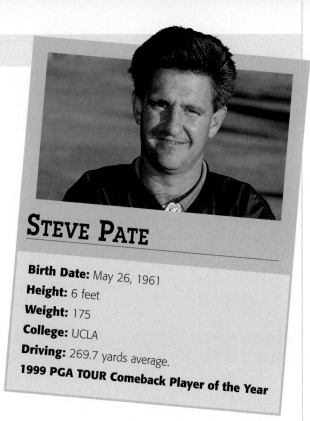

Steve Pate

Birth Date: May 26, 1961
Height: 6 feet
Weight: 175
College: UCLA
Driving: 269.7 yards average.
1999 PGA TOUR Comeback Player of the Year

My injuries from accidents are documented, but they had a positive effect on my swing. I have less moving parts now. My lack of hand strength no longer can make up for some of the bad positions I used to get into. As you get older, it hurts to swing as hard as you can.

When my swing goes off, the reasons are too many to list, but usually it starts at address, especially my posture or alignment. Basic fundamentals are important for all golfers. Grip, posture and alignment are areas I constantly work on during practice.

Being selected by Ben Crenshaw as a captain's pick for the victorious come-from-behind 1999 Ryder Cup Team was a great thrill for me. I was on the 1991 team but played only one match. Why only one? I was injured in a traffic accident on the way to the banquet and suffered a severely bruised hip.

—Steve Pate

Martin Hall

Martin Hall, one of the game's top instructors, provides his proven practice drills throughout this book. Hall appears regularly on the PGA TOUR Partners Video Series and has been selected as one of the 50 best golf instructors in the U.S.

1 EVALUATING YOUR DRIVES

All golfers have a gallery of their greatest drives on permanent display in their minds—those moments in time when everything meshed together perfectly and the ball was propelled long and accurately down the fairway.

Remember those shots, savor them, but be honest with yourself if you want to improve your game off the tee. Ask yourself truthfully, "Did those shots represent my average drive?"

Golf is a game of many elements, and consistency is at the top of the list. The key to determining how you can improve your game off the tee requires evaluating the components of your average drive: length, accuracy and flight pattern.

One way to evaluate and improve your drives is to pretend you played a round with our four PGA TOUR professionals featured in this book. As the five of you relax in the locker room after the round, here's your opportunity!

You have these four great pros at your disposal—ask them some direct questions on how you can improve your driving. Here are their straightforward answers—along with references of where to turn in this book for more help.

PRO:
JOHN DALY

QUESTION: HOW CAN I ACHIEVE LONGER DRIVES?

ANSWER:

The average drive on the PGA TOUR is in the 270-yard range. I average over 300 yards. Judging your average length based on TOUR standards would be unfair. The one thing I notice about my amateur partners is that their lack of distance usually comes from not correctly transferring their weight. Martin Hall has good drills to help you on pages 84 and 94.

—JD

PRO:
JOHN JACOBS

QUESTION: WHAT'S THE KEY TO IMPROVING MY DRIVING ACCURACY?

ANSWER:

The best way to improve accuracy is to work on alignment. Proper alignment to the target cures many swing faults. TOUR players are always working on their alignment as they practice, by hitting to specific targets. I'll show you how to improve your alignment on page 146. Martin Hall has some additional alignment tips on page 40.

—JJ

PRO: SCOTT McCARRON

QUESTION: HOW CAN I IMPROVE *BOTH* DRIVING DISTANCE AND ACCURACY?

ANSWER:

I enjoy helping my pro-am partners with their games. Driving distance can be improved by working on maintaining a wide swing arc, which increases clubhead speed. Accuracy can be improved by staying in balance throughout the swing. On page 128, I demonstrate my drill to help both areas of the game.

— SM

PRO: STEVE PATE

QUESTION: HOW FAR SHOULD I TAKE MY BACKSWING?

ANSWER:

Becoming a consistently good driver of the ball requires a backswing that allows very important timing elements to take place prior to impact. With a short backswing, it is virtually impossible for that to happen. It may be difficult, or even physically impossible, for you to get the club to a correct parallel position, but that is not necessary to become a consistently good driver. On page 129, Martin Hall has an angle-to-angle drill that will help you get the most from your backswing.

— SP

PRO:
JOHN DALY

QUESTION: WHAT'S THE RIGHT SWING TEMPO FOR ME?

ANSWER:

Scott McCarron and I have our own unique swing tempos, but we both are very long off the tee. Your swing tempo should match your normal body rhythm. Swinging fast is not the same as swinging hard, and doing so usually destroys any chance of developing length and accuracy. On page 142, Scott demonstrates how the "Little Circle/Big Circle" drill will help you understand the role of swing tempo.

—JD

PRO:
STEVE PATE

QUESTION: HOW SHOULD I FINISH MY SWING?

ANSWER:

Did you know that some teachers, to improve your swing, will suggest beginning in a follow-through position facing the target, then working your way backward? Look at our follow-through positions in Chapter 3.

—SP

PRO:
JOHN JACOBS

QUESTION: WHAT IS KEY TO CORRECTING MY SWING FAULTS?

ANSWER:

Understanding what causes the ball to fly along certain paths will help you understand how to correct your own swing faults. You can find some basic information on ball flight problems on page 132. Good drivers can work the ball in various directions. Martin Hall has some fade and draw drills on pages 167-172.

—JJ

PRO:
SCOTT MCCARRON

QUESTION: WHAT'S THE RIGHT BALL TRAJECTORY?

ANSWER:

Balls that fly too high or too low are distance robbers. Although sweeping your way through the ball will help produce the correct launch angle, you can find quick fixes to your problem by simply selecting a driver with a different loft. Page 154 explains how to choose the correct loft for your game.

—SM

2

SWING SEQUENCES

The action begins with high-speed photography showing the swing sequences of our four TOUR professionals. A golf swing takes 1.5 seconds to complete—one second to go from address to the top of the backswing, and a half-second to go from the top of the backswing to the follow-through. While that may seem fast, it's actually slower—and smoother—than you might imagine.

If you watched the players practice on the range at a PGA TOUR tournament, you would be surprised at how smooth and slow their body movements appear. Yet these players generate tremendous clubhead speed. For example, John Daly's clubhead speed has been clocked at 140 mph, but when you watch him in person, his swing is well-paced and smooth.

So, to get started on the road to driving with more power and precision, enjoy looking at some of the most powerful and efficient swings in golf.

JOHN DALY

Face On

Down the Line

JOHN JACOBS

Face On

Down the Line

Scott McCarron

Face On

Down the Line

STEVE PATE

Face On

Down the Line

3 ELEMENTS OF THE SWING

A TOUR professional's flowing, power-producing golf swing is like the movement of a fine Swiss watch. Both require that their many pieces fit and mesh together with precise timing, achieving high levels of performance. Unfortunately, just one faulty part can gum up the works.

So let's break down the golf swing into nine seperate components:

1. Address
2. Takeaway
3. Backswing extension
4. Top of the backswing
5. Transition to downswing
6. Downswing
7. Impact
8. Follow-through extension
9. Follow-through finish

With the exception of address, never think of any of these components as static or motionless. These only are junctures to pass through as the swing continues along its uninterrupted course. Even the follow-through finish is an action component because the swing stops naturally instead of a making a manipulated stop. Just as a watch must have its gears and levers mesh perfectly, the swing requires a precise timing of its own to link all the components together. This is something our four professionals do masterfully. Let's go inside the ropes for a close-up look.

ABOUT THIS SECTION

Now that you've seen detailed swing sequences of our four TOUR professionals, we will break down their swings into the nine key components. Here's what you will find.

- You will see each pro in two facing views of each of the nine components, and you will see all the pros before advancing to the next position. This makes it easy to compare what each player is doing in that position.

- You will see a close-up view of each swing component, just as if you were facing the pro and also watching from behind.

- We've included the pros' comments and added graphics where appropriate to help you work on your own swing.

At the conclusion of each swing component section, Martin Hall demonstrates some outstanding drills to help you master that phase of the swing. Some of these "Practice Tee" drills can be done at home using items you may have around the house. These "Practice Tee" sections make great references if something begins to go wrong with your swing.

A NOTE ON MOTION

Always think of the swing in terms of motion, not the static positions we have broken it into for instructional purposes. Refer back to chapter 2's swing sequences to keep the motion of the swing in the proper perspective.

ADDRESS

Think of your address position as the departure point for a great drive. Accuracy and distance require adhering to basic fundamentals that will allow a free-flowing swing.

As you go inside the ropes for a close-up view of our four professionals' address positions, they will share their thoughts and techniques to start you on the road to longer and more accurate drives off the tee.

At the end of the section, Martin Hall will demonstrate Practice Tee drills to improve your fundamentals.

Let's begin.

ADDRESS: JOHN DALY

As I set up to the ball my only swing thought is to grip it and rip it. But, having said that, I still have to incorporate basic fundamentals at address. Addressing the ball the same way every time helps build my consistency and confidence. I play my best when my confidence is high.

My head is behind the ball.

In my power position, I want a straight line to run from my left shoulder down through my left arm and the shaft. This pre-sets the same line that returns at impact.

My left shoulder is higher than my right.

In my interlocking grip, I want to feel light pressure in the last three fingers of my left hand. Notice that my thumb and index finger on my right hand are open. They remain open through my backswing and only close at the moment of impact when centrifugal force brings them together naturally.

My stance is wider than my shoulders. The width of my stance helps me maintain balance throughout my swing. The width of your stance should be shoulder-width apart, but you can experiment and adjust the width to fit your swing requirements.

The ball is positioned slightly off my left heel, which is the bottom of my swing arc. I have 60 percent of my weight on my right foot to promote loading my weight on my right side on the takeaway.

My target is an outcropping on the mountain bordering La Quinta's Mountain Course. It may look close, but it is well beyond my range. Be sure to have a specific target in mind before addressing the ball. It will help you accurately align yourself. My approach shot, and the opportunity to make birdie, will be dictated by where the ball lands.

I don't have textbook posture, but look at the spine angle from my head to the base of my spine and then to the ground. It shows I set a good spine angle to rotate freely back and through the ball.

My body shape and swing require more room, so I like to have my hands slightly farther away from my body than most professionals.

See how the thumb and index finger of my right hand are open at address. The only time I want my right hand getting into the shot is when my right thumb touches the palm at impact.

My knees are flexed. This athletic position will promote a powerful, balanced swing.

I'm aligned parallel to my target line.

I tee my ball so the top of the driver lines up with the ball's equator.

ADDRESS: JOHN JACOBS

Driving the ball with power and precision requires basic fundamentals. The best way to begin is to work on your pre-shot routine and address position.

Stand behind the ball and pick out a target, then take an address position so your swing can deliver the ball along that line. Grip, posture and ball position can be easily corrected, providing the basic foundation for a good swing.

Good ball strikers feel their head is steady throughout the swing. While a slight movement is inevitable, the head will remain the center of the swing if it's set behind the ball.

While my shoulders are parallel to my target line, they are not the same height. The right shoulder is lower.

My arm and shaft return to the ball in a straight line, but at address I do not pre-set them in that position.

I have a clubfitter build up the portion of the grip where my right hand goes. If the grip feels small in my right hand, my tendency is to hook the ball.

The V's of my hands point to inside my right shoulder.

The ball is positioned off my left heel, the bottom of my swing arc. I tee my ball a little higher because I want to catch the ball on the upswing to create the feeling I'm putting overspin on it.

My stance is narrower than John Daly's.

When I choose a target prior to addressing the ball, I basically know where the pin is on the hole. If the pin is on the right, for example, I pick a target on the left side of the fairway. For a left pin placement, I aim for a target on the right.

Hitting the fairway is not my primary concern unless it's the U.S. Senior Open and the rough is high. I'm more concerned with pin placement, knowing that if I miss the fairway it will only be by a couple of yards.

See how my chin points out to allow room for my shoulders to rotate under it. Have you misunderstood when someone told you to keep your head down? Locking your chin into your chest will throw your swing off plane as the shoulders bump your chin.

This is a pretty good athletic position for a senior golfer. The flex position encourages a smooth and powerful rotation.

My left thumb is not on top of the shaft but slightly to the side.

A closed stance—the left foot is closer to the target line than the right foot—helps get my weight to my right side easier. I don't play with a closed stance, but I practice this way to develop the feeling of weight transfer.

ADDRESS: SCOTT MCCARRON

Balance is an important key to my game, and it begins with a proper address position. If you swing in balance, you will usually hit the ball solidly. An out-of-balance swing causes you to work against yourself, resulting in lost clubhead speed, and a swing that is off plane.

I want the V's of both hands pointing to just inside or at my right shoulder. The grip should be relaxed and tension free. A brake is applied to clubhead speed if your grip is too tight. I grip the club before stepping into the ball.

I want my head behind the ball at address.

The width of my stance measures from the outside of my shoulders to the *inside* of my feet. Have you limited yourself in the past with a narrower stance, caused by lining up the outside of your shoulders with the *outside* of your feet?

The ideal address position should show a straight line extending down your left arm and the shaft.

I turn my left toe out slightly.

The ball should be positioned just off the inside of the left foot. This position allows the club to impact the ball square to your target line at maximum speed. Off-line shots may be the result of improper ball placement.

I want my weight distribution to be 50/50.

50%   50%

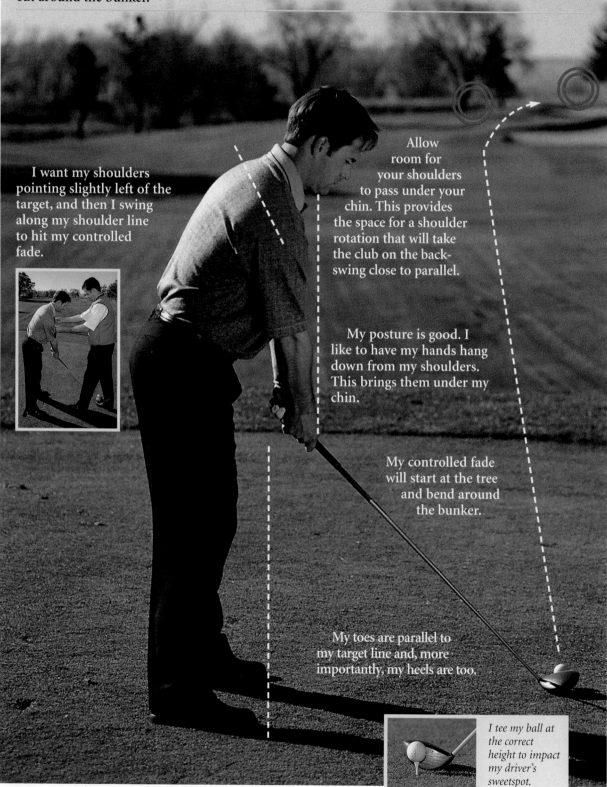

This fairway sets up perfectly for my favorite shot—a slight fade. I'm going to tee the ball on the right side of the tee box and aim it at the tree on the left and allow it to cut around the bunker.

I never have swing thoughts while I'm playing. My focus is from the ball to the target, and I trust my swing and let it go.

I want my shoulders pointing slightly left of the target, and then I swing along my shoulder line to hit my controlled fade.

Allow room for your shoulders to pass under your chin. This provides the space for a shoulder rotation that will take the club on the backswing close to parallel.

My posture is good. I like to have my hands hang down from my shoulders. This brings them under my chin.

My controlled fade will start at the tree and bend around the bunker.

My toes are parallel to my target line and, more importantly, my heels are too.

I tee my ball at the correct height to impact my driver's sweetspot.

ADDRESS: STEVE PATE

I have less moving parts in my swing than I did in college. After my injuries over the past few years, my swing fundamentals have improved because I no longer have the hand strength to compensate for the bad positions I used to get into.

My swing is geared to getting the ball in play by hitting the type of shot that matches the hole. That's why I like to say my normal shot with a driver is either a draw or fade, whichever the hole requires.

A good fundamental is to have your head behind the ball at address. If your head is forward of the ball, it's forced to move dramatically during the swing. Excessive head movement makes it difficult to return to the ball with power.

Have you noticed how all of us have a lower right shoulder at address? Check yourself in the mirror to work on this address position.

In this proper address position, a line can be drawn that goes straight down my left arm and the shaft. See how the same line is re-created at impact.

I placed tees in the V's of both hands to illustrate how they point to my right shoulder. If you slice the ball, those tees likely would be pointing left of your right shoulder. That is a weak grip.

With a driver, you need a wider stance. The outside of each foot is on line with my shoulders, allowing me to create a wide swing arc.

My weight is evenly distributed and over the balls of both feet. My feet are both slightly flared out to help my body rotate back and forth.

I address the ball on the toe of the club. I fought the shanks as a kid, and this helps me avoid that problem. Centrifugal force makes up the difference at impact.

This windy, wintry day at Wood Ranch in Simi Valley means I must factor the wind into this tee shot. I plan to hit a draw back into the wind, so I'm going to set my bodyline to where I want the ball to start. With a crosswind, I prefer to work the ball back into the wind, so it lands softer and stays in the fairway.

My body is flexed and relaxed at address. From this position, I could be taking snaps as the UCLA quarterback. Your weight should be over the balls of the feet. Check this by rocking back and forth, feeling the weight.

Fans at PGA TOUR tournaments often think I'm making a practice swing when they see this ball position. I use this position only when the ball is on a tee, not on the ground.

My club is aimed at my target. The rest of my body—shoulders, hips and feet—are aimed slightly right, on the line where the draw will begin.

THE GRIP

Nearly all the golfers I've taught are what I call "palm grippers," who incorrectly hold the club in the palm of the left hand. They immediately have two strikes against them: a slice-producing grip; and gaps that require a tight, power-restricting hold on the club. This combination eliminates both accuracy and distance.

The correct grip—I'll show you special left thumb placements for accuracy and distance shortly—has the club more in the fingers, with the heel pad sitting on top and the left thumb off to the side of the club. The photo lesson demonstrates this technique.

LEFT HAND AT YOUR SIDE

The easiest way to properly position your left hand on the club is to grip your club with your left hand resting by your trouser pocket. Try standing behind the ball, eye your target, and then take your grip.

CORRECT LEFT HAND CHECK   ### *ACROSS THE FINGER GRIP*

If you are correctly gripping the club with your fingers, you should be able to place a tee between the top of the shaft and the base of the palm pad. Your palm pad needs to be on top of the club, not the side. The left thumb should be more on the right side of the shaft.

The club will correctly lie across your open fingers for support.

POINT THE TEES TO 1 O'CLOCK

Your right hand grips the club lower on the shaft. It should rest only on the left thumb. To check your grip, put a tee between the thumb and forefinger of each hand. Both tees should be pointing to the 1 o'clock position. I prefer the clock reference, instead of thinking in terms of strong or weak grips or where the V's are pointing.

THE INTERLOCKING GRIP

John Daly and Jack Nicklaus both prefer an interlocking grip. The key is to be sure that it's interlocking, not "interloose."

INCORRECT "INTERLOOSE" GRIP

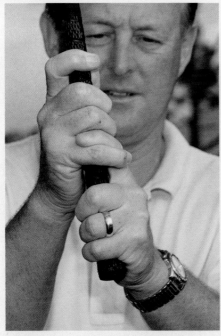

CORRECT INTERLOCKING GRIP

The space between the hands is the incorrect interpretation of an interlocking grip.

If you use the interlocking grip, it's important that it's a lock. Your fingers should be closed without gaps between the hands.

INTERLOCK CHECK

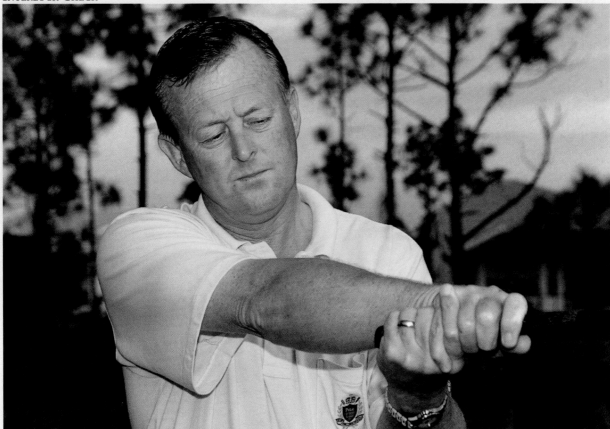

If you use the interlocking grip, give it periodic maintenance checks like this.

Elements of the Swing: Address

SHORT THUMB EQUALS MORE DISTANCE

Members in search of more distance should take advantage of the hinge in the left wrist. The shorter the left thumb in your grip, the more wrist flex you can have. A short left thumb promotes wrist action, which in turn creates speed. It also promotes a hook, which is beneficial if you tend to slice.

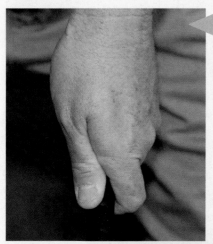

To encourage additional distance, try placing your left thumb about the same distance down the shaft as your forefinger. Notice that the thumb is still slightly on the side of the shaft.

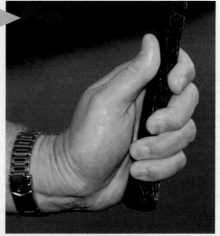

A shorter thumb allows more wrist flexibility, which promotes more speed in your swing, and additional distance.

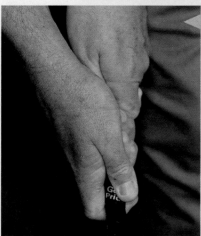

You will not see your left thumb "peeking out" as you look down your grip.

LONG THUMB EQUALS MORE ACCURACY

If you are satisfied with your distance but disappointed with your accuracy, try a long left thumb. A long thumb tightens up the left wrist and the forearm, which should produce a slight fade and a more accurate drive.

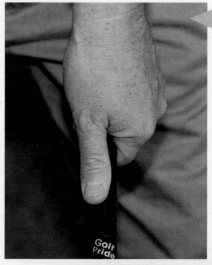

To improve your driving accuracy, extend the left thumb farther down the shaft. Notice the thumb is still slightly more on the side of the shaft.

A longer thumb limits wrist hinge. With less hinge, the wrists won't move as freely during the swing. While some swing speed is sacrificed, accuracy improves.

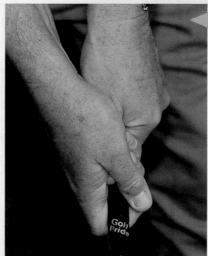

You should see the left thumb peeking out, if you use the long thumb grip for accuracy.

GRIP PRESSURE

Assuming that you're gripping the club correctly but still slicing, hold the club lighter and become more relaxed in the wrists. If you hook the ball, firm up your grip and wrists.

Lighter grip pressure allows the clubhead to turn over in the impact area, producing a more right-to-left ball flight. Firming grip pressure achieves the opposite. Whichever grip pressure you utilize, it needs to remain constant throughout the swing. Because more members probably slice than hook, try this wrist flexibility drill to encourage lighter grip pressure.

Correct grip pressure goes beyond your hands. It also involves relaxing the wrists and elbows. If you need to lighten up to create more swing speed, soft wrists and soft elbows will create more speed than firm wrists and firm elbows.

Hold your club out in front of you and make small circles to the left and then back to the right. The key is to make your wrists as relaxed as they can be. You want your hands to feel like clamps, but your wrists to be free.

WAGGLE FOR FLEXIBILITY

Pre-shot routines should include something that encourages wrist flexibility before the backswing begins. During all the years I worked for Jack Nicklaus, I never saw him hit a ball before waggling the club. The key is to know how to waggle.

Be sure to always waggle the club with your wrists on the swing plane the club needs to stay on.

I use this piece of wood with a ball in the back to provide the feeling of what I want my pre-swing waggle to accomplish. Using a sledge and pretending there is a nail on the back of the ball, I want both my waggle, and later my intent to strike the ball, to drive the nail through the ball. I'll use the sledge in the impact chapter drills to really help you develop this feeling.

Elements of the Swing: Address

KNEE FLEX

Having good posture also requires having flex in the knees. The question is how much? Try this jumping drill to develop a feeling for how much flex is right for you.

Bounce, or jump up and down, from your address position to develop a feeling for knee flex. Pre-setting your knee flex encourages athletic movement back and through the ball as you swing. It also helps to hold your spine angle constant.

ALIGNMENT

You can have a perfect grip and posture, but if your alignment is faulty it's impossible to hit an accurate drive. Correct alignment is perhaps the No. 1 fundamental that TOUR professionals work on when they practice.

The pros provided some excellent tips as you analyzed their address positions. I have a few more alignment checks (at right) to help launch your drives on the correct line. But first you need to build a practice station (below).

MARTIN'S DOG LEASH PRACTICE STATION

I use two dog leashes with clips on the ends to build a parallel line station. Attach tees to the clips to anchor the leashes, and separate the lines about a foot. The parallel lines will help you work on alignment and other phases of your swing.

PARALLEL SHOULDER CHECK

You aim with your shoulders. They have more to do with the path of the swing than your feet. To ensure your shoulders are parallel to the target lines, place your driver across your chest. Although the shoulders are tilted, the shaft must be parallel to the target line if you want to eliminate your slice.

We will show you how to work the ball in a later chapter, but for now if you are trying to correct a big slice, line up your shoulders parallel to the target line.

PARALLEL EYES CHECK

Hold your driver up to the bridge of your nose. The line of the club through your eyes should be parallel to the target line. In our practice station, the two parallel lines make that easy to see.

If your head is off line, then the shaft will not be parallel, and you will begin the swing off balance. The head must be set in the correct position so you can properly rotate your upper body around it.

POSTURE

If you want to drive the ball a long way, your posture should not be set up perpendicular to the ground. Instead of having your spine straight up and down, it should be angled away from the target. You will be looking at the back of the ball, like all good drivers.

With the top of your swing angled away from the target, your right shoulder is lowered. You need this angled posture to turn and get behind the ball and create weight transfer. I have three drills to help you set the perfect posture.

TILTED SPINE ANGLE DRILL

1 Begin by putting your driver straight down the center of your body.

2 Bend forward so the clubhead goes between your legs. While holding the club tightly, tilt your upper body away from the target until the clubhead contacts your upper left leg.

3 The spine angle away from the target allows me to see the back of the ball, as demonstrated in this posterior view.

UPHILL DRILL

To get the feel of driving with this tilted spine angle, make practice swings behind the tee from an uphill lie.

1 O'CLOCK POSTURE DRILL

You want to bend forward from the hips about 30 degrees. That's about the same as the distance between 12 o'clock and 1 o'clock on a clock face. That's how I try to picture it.

The spine is S-shaped, so you should have some natural curvature to it.

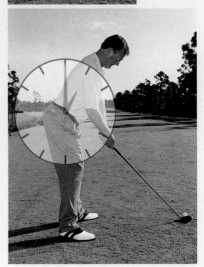

My chin is away from my chest as I look down at the ball.

Elements of the Swing: Address

BALL POSITION: BOTTOM OF THE SWING ARC

Ball position has nothing to do with the position of your feet, and everything to do with being at the bottom of your swing arc at impact. This is the impact position and the only spot where the clubface is squared to the target line.

A ball position slightly back of the arc bottom will result in a slightly open clubface, while a position slightly forward results in a closed clubface. Both incorrect ball positions translate into off-line shots.

Teeing your ball on line with the left shoulder joint consistently positions it correctly at the bottom of the swing arc. That means your driver will consistently be square to the target line at impact.

Regardless if you have a wide stance, like John Daly, or a narrow one, always place the ball off your left shoulder joint. Thinking in terms of foot position can get you into trouble.

In a narrow stance (above), my shoulder joint would be off my left heel. In a wider stance (left), the position of the shoulder joint dictates the ball is positioned farther back.

ELEMENTS OF THE SWING

TAKEAWAY

If your golf swing were a journey, the takeaway would be the equivalent of determining which way to turn out of your driveway. The first few feet of the golf swing are that vital for correctly arriving at your ultimate destination—more powerful (longer) and more precise (accurate) drives.

One point our professionals will stress is the role that correct weight transfer plays. Participating in pro-ams during PGA TOUR events, our pros see various weight transfer interpretations. In this section, as their swings begin, they'll demonstrate the proper way it should be done.

Martin Hall's Practice Tee drills, using the practice station built in the previous section, show how to take the club back through the gate to stay on-plane.

The takeaway has begun.

TAKEAWAY: JOHN DALY

On the takeaway, I begin the process of coordinating various body parts into a fluid swing. It is essential to create a wide swing arc for the clubhead to follow. I begin this by sweeping my club away from the ball.

A slight wrist angle develops as the club starts back. My hands are about in the same position, but a slight rotation of the forearm is causing this to occur. The shaft no longer is part of the same straight line with my left arm as it was at address. Compare this view to John Jacobs' takeaway.

My hips don't begin turning at this point of my takeaway. They are still parallel to the target line. I want them to offer some resistance to my big upper body turn.

The weight continues transferring to my right side. You should feel it increase on your right instep as the club goes back.

By keeping the club low to the ground, I begin working early on my extension. Think of this as a sweeping motion, like taking a broom back.

While growing up in Arkansas, I didn't have a lot of friends my age who played golf. I played with older guys and out drove them. They would get mad at me at first, but they eventually got over it.

My swing really hasn't changed much over the years. My accuracy statistics are not the best, but I would rather have a 50-yard shot to a par-4 out of the light rough, instead of a 150-yard shot from the fairway. Taking advantage of my length boosts my confidence.

See how my right thumb is away from the shaft at takeaway. I like to feel the left hand taking the club back.

The route to a powerful drive takes the club back on an inside track and brings it back the same way. This lets the clubface square naturally to the ball at impact.

Elements of the Swing: Takeaway

TAKEAWAY: JOHN JACOBS

The takeaway is a crucial point in my swing. My tendency is to slightly reverse pivot by allowing my left knee to point down and absorb some weight rather than shifting my weight to my right side properly.

As you look at my takeaway, see how I make a one-piece movement away from the ball. My hands, arms and shoulders all work together to sweep the clubface away. I often see my pro-am partners initiate the swing by picking up the club. When they think of clubhead speed, they believe it comes from swinging their arms quickly; they forget about the role the lower body plays. Start your swing motion correctly and practice transferring your weight to the right side.

The triangle formed by my hands, arms and shoulders has taken the shaft away from the ball in a one-piece movement with very few other moving parts. The straight line down my left arm and shaft still is intact. The more parts that move, the harder it is to coordinate all their movements properly.

My weight is transferring properly to my right side.

I keep the clubhead low to the ground on the takeaway to help begin my swing arc extension.

JOHN SAYS:

I started playing golf when I was three years old. My father was the head of Parks and Recreation in Montebello, CA, outside of Los Angeles. The golf course was in his jurisdiction, so his office was in the clubhouse. My older brother, Tommy, and I have been around golf our entire lives.

When Tommy joined the PGA TOUR, I played practice rounds with Arnold Palmer, Dow Finsterwald and Tony Lema. I noticed how they handled themselves on the course and how they approached playing. That was more beneficial to me than anything.

S wing the club away from the ball smoothly. A good golf swing takes one second to go from address to the top of the backswing. Practice swinging your club back by saying "one thousand one" out loud.

It's a surprising amount of time, proving you don't have to rush to make a complete backswing. As you will see later, a complete backswing does not mean you have to go all the way to parallel.

Maintain your body flex as you start back. You should be relaxed and have a light grip on your club. Keep all tension out of your swing. A relaxed body can turn easier than a rigid one.

The clubhead must always swing away from the ball on an inside track and return to it along the same path.

TAKEAWAY: SCOTT McCARRON

Extending my swing arc and staying in balance were vital to me in averaging nearly 289 yards in driving distance. While I have a one-piece takeaway too, we chose a photo that is one frame later into the swing than the one used for John Daly. It shows that when I reach the same shaft/triangle position as John, my clubhead is almost two feet past my right foot; at the same shaft/triangle position, John's clubhead is just passing his right foot.

I need this extra extension to allow my clubhead to gain distance-producing clubhead speed. The wider the swing arc, the more room it has to increase its speed. At 5-foot-10 and 165 pounds, I need every advantage to keep up with the big guys.

One frame earlier in my swing sequence you would see I swing my hands, arms and shoulders away from the ball in the same one-piece takeaway you saw in John Jacobs' swing. But in this photo, the angle of the line on my shaft looks similar to John Daly's (below). I work on extension all the time, and will have some exercises to share with you later.

All good drivers transfer weight to the right side as they swing the club back. SENIOR PGA TOUR player Ed Dougherty explains it properly when he says the weight follows your hands.

Notice how far I sweep the club away from the ball before the wide swing arc naturally lifts it into the air.

Don't begin rotating your shoulders and hips at the same time. Begin the one-piece takeaway with your hands, arms and shoulders. Your hips will turn later, but they need to slightly resist to build the body torque that helps unwinding back to the ball once you reach the top of your takeaway.

My hands are hanging down inside my chin line as I take the club back. The rotating shoulders will have plenty of room to clear under my chin as they take the club back to parallel.

For the controlled fade, my feet are parallel to the target line and I take the club back inside the line. On the downswing you will see how I swing along my open shoulder line.

Elements
of the
Swing:
Takeaway

TAKEAWAY: STEVE PATE

As you get older, it hurts to swing as hard as you can. Fundamentals really become even more important. Experience has taught me that the harder the golf course, the more important it is to just put the ball in play off the tee.

The wind was gusting to 40 mph the day we shot this sequence, so I'm really trying to stay within myself as I make my swing. Maintaining a steady base while shifting my weight properly is important in strong winds. Playing on less-than-perfect days helps you improve because you learn to stay within yourself and be more deliberate with your movements.

My takeaway begins much the same as that of the other pros; but the straight line of my shaft and arm angles slightly after the clubhead passes my right foot.

My knee flex clearly shows as I sweep the club away on my take-away. Notice how I maintain the flex as you look at other positions in my swing.

I want the clubhead to skim the ground as long as possible. This ensures a wide swing arc.

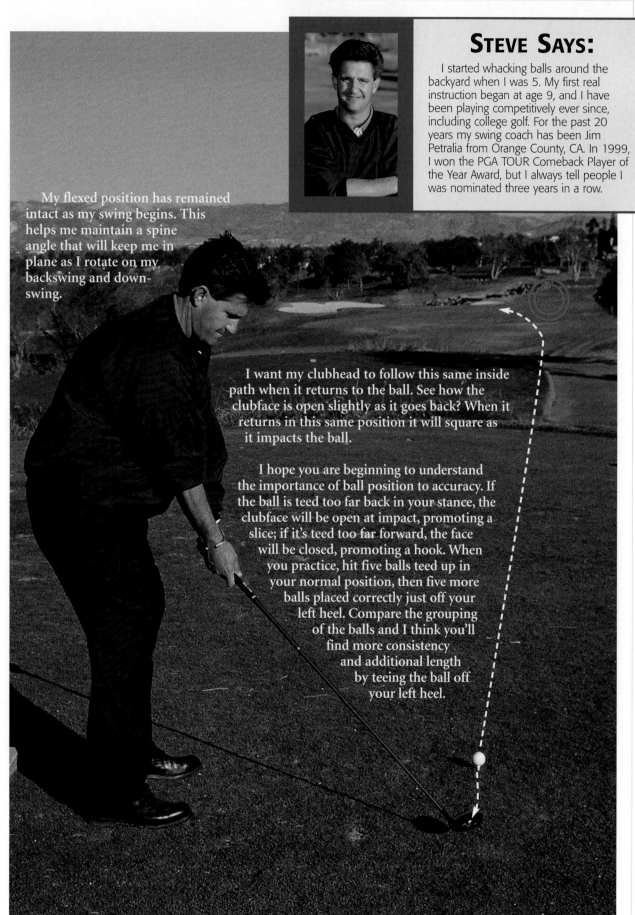

I started whacking balls around the backyard when I was 5. My first real instruction began at age 9, and I have been playing competitively ever since, including college golf. For the past 20 years my swing coach has been Jim Petralia from Orange County, CA. In 1999, I won the PGA TOUR Comeback Player of the Year Award, but I always tell people I was nominated three years in a row.

My flexed position has remained intact as my swing begins. This helps me maintain a spine angle that will keep me in plane as I rotate on my backswing and down-swing.

I want my clubhead to follow this same inside path when it returns to the ball. See how the clubface is open slightly as it goes back? When it returns in this same position it will square as it impacts the ball.

I hope you are beginning to understand the importance of ball position to accuracy. If the ball is teed too far back in your stance, the clubface will be open at impact, promoting a slice; if it's teed too far forward, the face will be closed, promoting a hook. When you practice, hit five balls teed up in your normal position, then five more balls placed correctly just off your left heel. Compare the grouping of the balls and I think you'll find more consistency and additional length by teeing the ball off your left heel.

Elements of the Swing: Takeaway

PRACTICE TEE

The practice station we built to work on your address is also an invaluable tool to develop correct takeaway skills. This is where the swing plane begins, and we want to train our muscle memory to take the clubhead away from the ball consistently on the proper arc.

The pros have mentioned that a golf swing is a fluid movement, not posed positions. When it's time to actually drive your ball off the tee, your only focus should be on your target.

Practicing technical drills like these helps train your muscles and develop the feel you can rely on when you tee it up for real. Practicing techniques to develop feel gives you game improvement strategy, rather than a quick fix that will ultimately fail.

TAKEAWAY GATE DRILL

The key to this drill is to take the club away in a one-piece motion between poles placed on the parallel lines. This creates the beginning of the powerful swing arc.

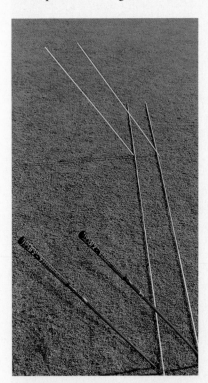

1 Using the parallel dog leash lines we set up in our practice station, place two shafts—or poles—that are at the same clubshaft angle on the takeaway side of the ball, and two shafts on the follow-through side.

Place the shafts on the inside parallel line and the outside parallel line, creating gates for the club to fit between as you practice.

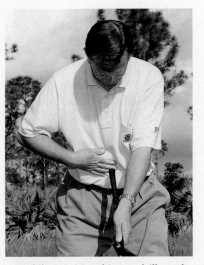

2 While practicing this gate drill to take the club away on the proper plane, you should feel the shaft is pointing to the middle of your body throughout the drill. The best way to develop this feeling is to grip down on the club until the shaft touches your abdomen.

3 Without using a ball, take the club away slowly so that it passes between the gates to about hip height. Keep the shaft touching your abdomen as you swing. This prevents a "flippy wrist" movement.

4 The driver head passes on plane through the gate. As you look at this down-the-line photo, try to visualize the circular swing plane the club will follow. This helps develop a circular feeling for your golf swing.

5 Swing forward, past where the ball would be teed, and allow the clubhead to pass through the gates on the other side, to about hip height. Practice this drill at home to train your muscles to feel the correct takeaway. Remember: Don't use a ball for this drill. Just concentrate on passing the clubhead through the gates.

PRACTICE RANGE TAKEAWAY DRILL

Let's take your new takeaway to the range and hit some balls. To reinforce the shaft pointing to your middle as you swing, you will need a short plastic pole that you can find at home improvement or hobby stores. Along with the dog leash, the plastic poles I'll be using in these drills are the least expensive training aids you'll ever find.

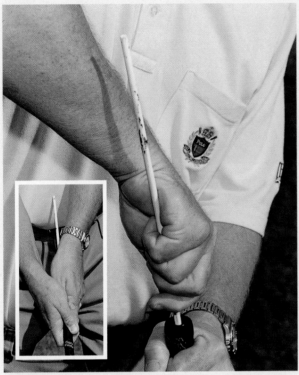

1 *Insert the pole—a stick can also be used—into the grip hole. The pole is for pointing purposes only and should not be pressed tightly against your abdomen.*

2 *Using the parallel line practice station, tee the ball between the parallel lines. The ball should be teed to line up with your left shoulder joint and the stick should be pointed at the center of your abdomen.*

3 *Keeping the pole pointed toward the center of your abdomen, swing the clubhead away to hip height along the same takeaway swing plane you previously practiced.*

4 *From the hip high position on the takeaway, swing through the ball along the swing plane you practiced. Finish the follow-through at hip height. Relax and feel the rhythm of your swing.*

Elements of the Swing: Takeaway

SENIOR GOLFER TAKEAWAY

For members, especially seniors, who want more driving distance but experience difficulty taking the club back due to hip tightness, here's a tip.

Begin by taking a normal stance with your feet parallel to the target line.

Move your right foot slightly back of its original set-up position (inset photo, above right). Don't move the line of your shoulders (right). They must remain parallel to the target line. This position makes it easier to rotate your body away from the ball.

You will be able to stay on plane as your backswing length increases. Extra distance off the tee should result.

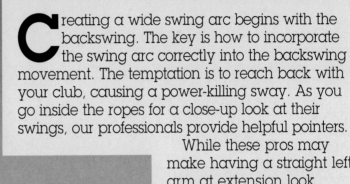

BACKSWING EXTENSION

Creating a wide swing arc begins with the backswing. The key is how to incorporate the swing arc correctly into the backswing movement. The temptation is to reach back with your club, causing a power-killing sway. As you go inside the ropes for a close-up look at their swings, our professionals provide helpful pointers.

While these pros may make having a straight left arm at extension look easy, that's not the case for every golfer. Try extending your arm as straight as it can. Don't become discouraged if you can't duplicate their positions. Any extension improvement you can incorporate will create a wider swing arc than you had previously.

On the Practice Tee, Martin Hall demonstrates drills to show the hand positions on the backswing. You also will benefit from the pointing finger drill David Graham used while preparing for his eventual 1981 U.S. Open victory.

Turn the page and extend away.

BACKSWING EXTENSION: JOHN DALY

As we help you understand the various positions in your swings, it's important to emphasize that what you are seeing happens naturally. We don't make a concentrated effort to set the wrist cock, as you see in the main photo. It happens as a result of the momentum of the clubhead swinging back.

This is where grip and grip pressure enter. If you put a chokehold on the grip at address, the wrists and forearms will have too much tension to allow this natural wrist cock to occur. Relax your grip and the club can swing naturally into the necessary positions.

I still have the feeling that my left hand is taking the club back. My arms are extended as far as they can go. Clubhead momentum sets the wrists at a 90-degree angle.

My hips have not rotated back as far as my shoulders. Too much lower body rotation is just as bad as no rotation. Your hips should be pulled back by the rotating upper body, not turned purposely. Maintain a feeling of a little hip resistance while you turn and you will start to feel the torque build up.

From this view, you can see how my upper body has rotated more than my hips. My big shoulder turn has my back correctly facing the target.

I try to maintain a stiff right leg as a pivot point to turn around. Upper body rotation brought me to this point. I have not leaned to the right to extend, as some members may be doing. See how my chin is lined up with my instep?

As my weight continues to shift over to the right side, my left knee begins to bend.

My backswing goes beyond parallel, so two different photos of my extension are being shown to illustrate how I swing the club back.

In the smaller photo (below), I rotate my forearms open on the backswing, so it appears that I let the club get behind me. My swing plane is flat.

I have always had this swing and it works for me. I only get in trouble if I rush my takeaway. The key for me is to stay within my natural rhythm and just grip it and rip it.

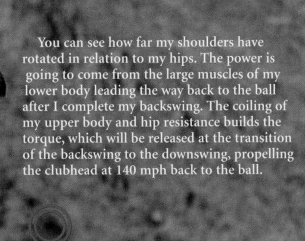

You can see how far my shoulders have rotated in relation to my hips. The power is going to come from the large muscles of my lower body leading the way back to the ball after I complete my backswing. The coiling of my upper body and hip resistance builds the torque, which will be released at the transition of the backswing to the downswing, propelling the clubhead at 140 mph back to the ball.

My swing plane looks flat with the club behind me in this position. However, it's only a midway point on my backswing, and the club continues up and back with good extension and on plane.

BACKSWING EXTENSION: JOHN JACOBS

I can't emphasize enough the importance of proper weight transfer. Weight is power, and wherever the weight goes, power follows. During extension, as the swing arc develops, the weight should be transferring to the back leg. If the weight stays on the forward leg, you won't have power to transfer back.

Practice in front of a mirror or videotape your swing to check on your weight shift. I see reverse pivots rob potentially good golfers of power because they don't understand how the weight shift should occur. This is one time when feeling you are shifting your weight properly is not enough. Make a visual check to verify it.

My arms are extending out, building a wide swing arc. The shaft is set at a 90-degree angle to my arms. This is a power backswing position.

I have a tendency to reverse pivot because my back is constantly bothering me; reverse pivoting eases the pressure. To combat this, I try to turn my left hip on the backswing.

As my swing revolves around my head, the weight has properly shifted over to the right side. The upper body should look as if it's directly over the lower body.

By turning my left hip, I'm trying to prevent it from going down and incorrectly absorbing weight that should be moving back. I practice turning my left hip to shift all of my weight to the right side. Then I pull through the ball with my left side on the downswing.

Sometimes I can get away with making a slight reverse pivot, but only because I drive the ball a long way. Consistency only comes by following good fundamentals. My backswing, as seen from this view, is building and storing the power that soon will be released as the clubhead returns to the ball.

This is a very good extension position. My shoulder is rotating under my chin and my back is facing the target. The angle of the club naturally occurred as the clubhead momentum brought it back.

The swing plane of my arc is around and up. Some members may be taking the club up but not around. A powerful golf swing comes down and around from inside the target line on the downswing, and continues around and up inside the target line during the follow-through. The only time the clubhead should be on the target line is when a square face impacts the ball.

The stick coming out of the bottom of my grip illustrates where I want the butt of the club pointing just before I reach the swing point of the main photo. I'm on a perfect swing plane when the stick points to the target line and right of the ball. The shaft-and-stick is a good visual reference to help understand the path your clubface should follow.

The correct weight transfer to my right side makes it possible to raise my left heel.

BACKSWING EXTENSION: SCOTT McCARRON

This position reveals how wide the swing arc will be because of my extension. I work hard at maintaining and strengthening my extension. The small photo (page 61) shows the ball extension drill I do with my coach, Todd Sones; I'll show you the complete extension-building drill for my entire swing on page 129.

Proper extension is achieved by extending the club out at a 90-degree angle. Increasing the angle farther, to say 180 degrees, would potentially increase the swing arc, but it would also promote what is called "casting" the club on the downswing, which is weak and ineffective.

Power is ignited through my lower body pulling the club back to the ball as my downswing reaches this position. The fastest clubhead speed comes from a pulling action, not a casting motion.

This is the 90-degree angle I want to set as my shoulder rotation and straight arm extends the club back. This extension sets up my swing for a powerful return to the ball.

My weight is correctly transferring over to my right side. The swing will revolve around a steady head that is in line with my body.

I have worked on getting my swing arc wide because a previous tendency brought the club too close to my body. I would jam it a little, and because the clubhead was slightly open at impact, the ball would flame out to the right without much power.

Unfortunately, photos can't show tempo as you analyze swings. Tempo and rhythm are essential to my game. My speed is a little slower going back. If my rhythm and tempo are good, I usually play well that day.

My back is to the target and my club is positioned properly for this point in my swing.

Placing a large beach ball between my legs, a two-pound ball between my forearms and a four-pound ball in my hands, I work on building and maintaining my extension with Todd.

BACKSWING EXTENSION: STEVE PATE

Here I am again battling 40 mph Simi Valley winds. This is a very good training situation in which to work on balance throughout my swing. Any motion out of balance will be magnified immediately.

My weight shift better be correct if I want the ball to make any headway to the target as I draw the club back into these swirling winds. The line proves it is. Even bundled up you can see I have the weight over my right instep and back in my stance where it belongs.

Both feet are still on the ground as I transfer my weight. I need a solid base to hit from in this wind.

So many things must happen in the golf swing that it would be impossible to deliberately coordinate them. Fortunately, you don't have to; they happen naturally. Relax your body, grip the club, set up in a good, athletic position, make a one-piece takeaway, and just swing the club. Your wrists will naturally arrive at this hinged position.

In this view, you can see my shoulder rotation has turned my back to the target while my hips have turned only slightly. I want a big upper body turn. The hips will turn, but not as much. If they do turn, I won't have the torque needed to ignite my downswing with the feeling of releasing a coiled spring.

To get to this position, I just swing the club back in my normal rhythm without thinking about the wind or technique.

I have retained my body flex and spine angle as the club swings away from the ball. The extension and wrist hinging are occurring on their own. This is a free-flowing motion.

PRACTICE TEE

While the swing arc must be extended to allow centrifugal force to build maximum clubhead speed, correct hand and arm positions are critical in allowing the clubhead to remain on plane. Here are some very good drills to help you establish the correct position for backswing extension.

POLE EXTENSION DRILL

You will need two shafts or poles to place at the driver shaft angle on the backswing and follow-through sides of our dog leash practice station. Insert them into the ground on the inside parallel line.

A longer version of the pole we inserted into your grip for the takeaway drills is also needed to help illustrate and reinforce the correct shaft position as the arms are parallel to the ground.

1 Begin by placing the pole on the right side of your body as you address the ball.

2 As you take the club away along the plane you practiced, allow it to swing to the top of the planted shaft. As the wrists hinge and the arms become parallel to the ground, the shaft should be pointing at the line and parallel to the shaft stuck in the ground.

3 In this down-the-line view, notice how the pole is pointing at the target line and the driver shaft is parallel to the shaft in the ground.

DAVID GRAHAM'S INDEX FINGER DRILL

This is the drill David Graham used before winning the 1981 U. S. Open at Merion Golf Club. Think of the index finger of your right hand as a gun as it points down the shaft. Its position will help you progress properly through your swing.

1 The right hand index finger is extended down the backside of the grip at address, pointing to the ball.

2 As you swing back, the finger points up toward the sky.

3 At impact, the finger again points at the ball as it did at address.

4 At follow-through extension, the finger points at the target.

5 As you begin reaching the follow-through completion, the right index finger is aimed toward the sky. You may not win the U.S. Open as David did, but this drill could make you the driving distance and accuracy leader when playing with your buddies.

TOP OF THE BACKSWING

The goal for the top of your backswing should be to swing back far enough to allow all the timing elements to come together at impact. Strive to achieve the proper length and swing tempo that works best for you.

Most TOUR players consider their bodies to be more important tools for good golf than their clubs. Stretching and strengthening certain muscle groups help lengthen the extension of backswings and ease rotational movements (find those healthy stretches in Chapter 7).

In the Practice Tee, Martin Hall demonstrates a unique drill with a book to get you to the top of your backswing correctly.

Now let's see why a good backswing can help you achieve top clubhead speed at impact.

TOP OF THE BACKSWING: JOHN DALY

My backswing has always gone far beyond parallel because I don't try to control it. The length of my backswing doesn't concern me as long as my tempo is not rushed. I'm fully coiled and ready to initiate the transition back to the ball.

My weight has shifted to my right side. I'm coiled around my head, and my chin is on line with my instep. This is perfect weight distribution.

My shoulders have made a maximum turn while my hips have exerted some resistance. The wrinkles in my shirt are a good visual example of the torque I have built in my backswing. This is a very powerful position, just waiting to be released.

My shoulder rotates under my chin. Even though some contact is made, my head remains steady. If your head moves back and forth as you swing, it will be difficult to get back to the ball without making a swing compensation.

When I'm fully loaded up on my backswing, it feels as if my right knee locks. It does not move. My swing is so long that I need to have this locked leg as a solid base.

This is not exactly a textbook position for the top of the backswing, but it has worked for me. I'm sure it will shorten as I get older. One interesting point you should note in this photo is that my feet and clubface are both parallel to the target line.

TOP OF THE BACKSWING: JOHN JACOBS

The top of my backswing is proof that you do not need to bring the club to parallel to lead the SENIOR PGA TOUR in driving distance. My backswing is a little shorter than it was when I was younger. The key is a wide swing arc, transferring the weight properly, and staying in rhythm during the swing to produce maximum centrifugal force.

I stay extended through the top of my backswing, maximizing the shape of my swing arc. The shoulders are fully coiled and ready to follow the lower body and release back to the ball.

My hips have barely turned in comparison to my shoulders. As the torque increases in my backswing, that signals to me that it's time to initiate the downswing.

This is the line to strive for to ensure proper weight transfer—a straight line that begins at your chin, goes through your right leg and ends at the instep of your right foot. The weight should be felt on the instep of the right foot.

At the top of your backswing you need to be fully coiled and on plane. You can visualize the path my club will take as it accelerates back to the ball. The shaft is flexing as the weight of the clubhead continues back for a fraction of a second, even though I've stopped my backswing,

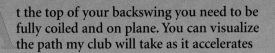

I posed for this photo with a stick in my grip to illustrate how the shaft relates to the target line. It should be parallel. Because I don't get the shaft parallel to the ground on my back-swing, it's okay for the clubhead to point slightly left of the target.

When you rotate John Daly to a parallel position at the top of his backswing, his shaft is parallel to the line. This is another position you can check in your mirror at home.

TOP OF THE BACKSWING: SCOTT MCCARRON

All elements should now be incorporated into your fully coiled backswing. A good backswing should have the hands high and over the right part of the body. Working on my extension allows me to rotate even farther back so my hands are high and more over my center.

My hips have been naturally pulled to their position and haven't over rotated, which would be a power leak. I'm totally in balance and ready to release back to the ball.

See how the flex of my clubhead continued beyond parallel. Now I'm ready to initiate my transition.

The weight should be transferred fully over the instep of my right foot. The shoulder rotation was around a steady head.

Balance is evident, as I've kept the distance between my knees the same during the backswing. The extension ball drill I'll show you on pages 128-129 helps develop this feeling.

I have remained in balance with a solid base. The weight transferred to the right side without moving or lifting my feet.

Being long is good, but being long and accurate is wonderful. Accuracy begins when you select your target and properly align yourself to it. At the top of my backswing, I want the shaft parallel to both the ground and the target line. Achieve this position consistently with your swing and we may be teeing off together in next year's Masters.

If my shoulders have rotated 90 degrees to the ball, my hips have rotated about 40 degrees. The difference between the two develops the torque that will powerfully release my stored energy.

The stick in the end of my shaft illustrates how my shaft is parallel to the ground and to my target.

TOP OF THE BACKSWING: STEVE PATE

I'm still out here in the wind. In spite of the blustery conditions, I have maintained my balance and completed my backswing. I've created the opportunity for centrifugal force to take over and follow a wide swing arc back to the ball.

This is a good example of how transferring my weight properly makes it possible to have my chin over my right side. Notice how the top of my body is not leaning, but is directly over the lower body.

My hands are high and over the right side of my body. Not as far as Scott McCarron's, but still a very good position. The shaft is parallel to the ground and the weight of the clubhead has flexed the shaft. I'm ready to release.

I have retained my body flex at the top of my backswing and I'm still parallel to the target line, which is where I want the ball to start before it draws back toward the target. If you are faced with windy conditions, it's important to relax and forget about the wind. Play intelligently and factor the wind direction into your target alignment.

A smooth, rhythmic swing is always a good idea, especially when the wind is blowing. Maintaining your balance is important. Just think how easy this will be on a calm day.

Even at the top of my backswing I have maintained body flex and the same spine angle. Consistency is encouraged when you can maintain a constant spine angle to rotate around, both on the backswing and downswing.

EXTENSION BOOK DRILL

This drill will help train your hands to find the correct path along the swing plane, past extension and all the way to the top of the backswing. Just have the cover face out at the top!

It's a also a good idea to practice the free-flowing swing as new positions are incorporated. This drill even shows you where the book face should be as you swing down and through the impact position to follow-through.

1 Begin this drill with a book, binder or PGA TOUR Partners magazine between the palms of your hands.

2 As you begin the backswing extension, the cover rotates parallel to the target line.

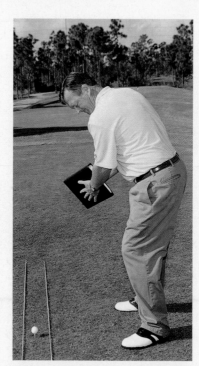

3 Notice the position of the book's cover at the top of my backswing. It is parallel to the target line but tilted onto the swing plane angle.

4 As I swing down toward impact, the book is returning to its original address position, with the cover facing the target. Notice how it is approaching the ball from the powerful inside track.

5 As I follow-through, the back cover is now parallel to the target line and tilted onto the swing plane.

TRANSITION TO DOWNSWING

"Coiled like a spring and waiting to be powerfully released" is the ideal description of a backswing. How you begin unleashing this stored up energy is the key. If your shoulders begin the transition to the downswing, all the good things you have worked on to get to the top will be in vain.

Your hips *must* lead the way back to the ball, as our professionals demonstrate. To really appreciate this movement, compare the large transition photos to the smaller ones showing all the pros at the top.

In Martin Hall's Practice Tee, try the "leftfield hip slide" transition drill to get your downswing started correctly.

Time to let your hips lead the way.

TRANSITION TO DOWNSWING: JOHN JACOBS

My transition ignites with a feeling of pulling back to the left side. As you look at this position, it's pretty obvious I delay the transfer of weight until my left knee straightens and can support it.

If you want to stay on plane, beginning the transition from the ground up is the only correct way. My hips actually begin turning as the upper body is in the final microseconds of the backswing. This increases the amount of torque. A downswing may produce power, but it should be smooth, and the clubhead should reach maximum acceleration at impact.

This is a powerful extended position that guarantees my swing arc will be wide. Grip pressure should always be light so that wrist hinging and unhinging can occur naturally.

The shaft reflects the beginning of centrifugal force as it bends from two different movements. As the hips begin their rotation, the upper body has just reached the top of the backswing and the clubhead weight is causing a slight curvature in the shaft as it reacts.

Weight is power and I delay transferring it until my left leg can properly support it.

Hip rotation should begin your downswing.

Notice how my left knee position has changed and now will support the body weight as I transfer it. The width of the gap between my knees will keep me in balance as I start back.

This view clearly shows that my transition motion begins with my knees and hips. You can visualize my swing plane back to the ball. My hips have rotated almost parallel to the target line; notice the room I'm going to have as I rotate my upper body through at impact.

The flex of the shaft caused by the clubhead shows the direction the hips are pulling the upper body. This bend should help you visualize the swing plane back to the ball.

Maintaining this wrist hinge and extended left arm will allow a free flowing, power-producing swing as centrifugal force takes over.

My chin remains pointed out, allowing the shoulders to rotate freely back on the downswing.

TRANSITION TO DOWNSWING: SCOTT MCCARRON

Some members may want to rush to get back to the ball on their downswing, but I have a slow feeling. Bob Murphy makes a deliberate pause at the top of his backswing prior to starting back. While I don't pause, I do feel a brief hesitation as my upper body lags behind.

This lagging creates power as the lower body movement starts the downswing. My quick hip rotation creates the opportunity to stay pretty wide and make up the speed with the lower body.

Good extension continues along with my wrist angle.

My belt buckle shows how far my hips have rotated back toward the ball while my upper body lags behind. My fast hip speed allows me to stay wide and catch up. Because of the centrifugal force I've built up, my clubhead speed will exceed 120 mph.

As my lower body begins the transition, my weight begins to shift back to my left side. The line shows it has moved about a foot away from my instep toward the target.

As I start the downswing transition, I remain in balance. The weight will shift over smoothly.

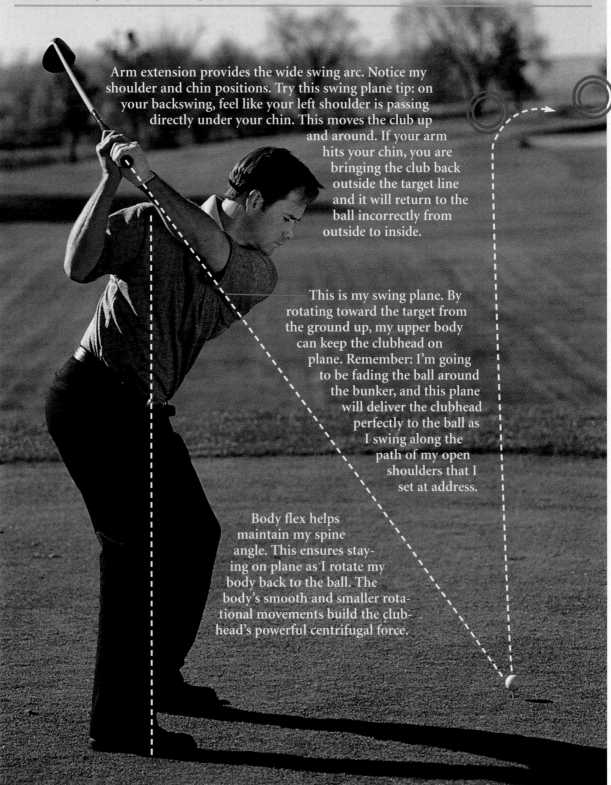

As my hips start to uncoil, I start to feel resistance in my midsection and right hip, signaling when to begin the transition to my downswing. I try to feel a slight pause at the top of my backswing as I maintain my wide swing arc. This helps me smoothly accelerate while staying on plane.

Arm extension provides the wide swing arc. Notice my shoulder and chin positions. Try this swing plane tip: on your backswing, feel like your left shoulder is passing directly under your chin. This moves the club up and around. If your arm hits your chin, you are bringing the club back outside the target line and it will return to the ball incorrectly from outside to inside.

This is my swing plane. By rotating toward the target from the ground up, my upper body can keep the clubhead on plane. Remember: I'm going to be fading the ball around the bunker, and this plane will deliver the clubhead perfectly to the ball as I swing along the path of my open shoulders that I set at address.

Body flex helps maintain my spine angle. This ensures staying on plane as I rotate my body back to the ball. The body's smooth and smaller rotational movements build the clubhead's powerful centrifugal force.

TRANSITION TO DOWNSWING: STEVE PATE

All of us agree that you start your transition back to the ball from the ground up. Your feet don't move, but they do feel the weight shifting as it transfers from your right instep forward toward your target.

The reason for not turning your hips all the way back becomes evident at transition. If the shoulders rotate away from the ball to a 90-degree angle and the hips rotate only half as much, you wind up your upper body like a spring. As the hips start back first while the shoulders are just reaching their final backswing position, those shoulders may be pulled slightly but still have all their unwinding to do.

As the arms pull down, the clubhead follows along its wide swing arc and gains speed. The hips need to turn past the impact area first to provide the upper body with the clearance it needs. It may look like a large lead, but later swing photos will show you how fast the upper body catches up.

As my transition begins, my weight begins to move smoothly back toward the target. The weight is now off my right instep and moving left.

Hip rotation leads the way. In windy conditions, it's important to make smooth movements to stay on plane.

Feel the weight shift in the balls of your feet.

Extension, body flex and balance play the most important roles in my swing:

- Extension creates a wide swing arc.

- Body flex creates an athletic position that maintains my spine angle.

- Balance comes from making a smooth body rotation that will create the centrifugal force I need to drive the ball.

- A proper swing plane will allow you to feel totally in balance. If the club goes too far outside or inside, the weight will adversely affect your balance.

- Practice trying to re-create our body positions in your mirror at home.

The bend in my shaft shows the direction the club is being pulled as my hips lead the downswing.

Even if you can't extend your left arm this straight on your backswing, you can still get your maximum extension by not allowing it to collapse.

My body flex and spine angle remain the same. I can't emphasize enough how important this is to an athletic golf swing. Golf is a rotational sport, and when you rotate on the backswing you have to follow that same rotation on the downswing to powerfully and accurately drive the golf ball.

PRACTICE TEE

Now that you've made a perfect backswing and are perfectly positioned to initiate your return to the ball, a little baseball terminology will get you on your way to an effective downswing.

LEFTFIELD HIP SLIDE TRANSITION DRILL

This drill helps initiate proper movement of your hips back to the ball. That's what brings the arms down. I don't believe you bring them down separately. Just as our professionals demonstrated, the lower body initiates the downswing and triggers the rotation of the shoulders and arms toward the ball.

1 Begin this drill from the address position in order to provide some movement to the top of the backswing so you can create the transition. Place one of your newly purchased poles—or sticks—from behind your right heel towards your left toe. The stick represents the direction and distance you should feel your hips moving—toward leftfield on the downswing.

2 Swing the club to the top of your backswing along the same plane you have been practicing.

3 Start your downswing by moving your hips along the diagonal line represented by the stick. If you were playing baseball, this would be a sliding motion toward leftfield. As your hips move laterally, they bring the arms down automatically.

While this drill will correctly start the transition, it's an exaggerated movement compared to our professionals. But the point is to develop the feeling of having your hips move laterally, not just turning back.

This lateral movement will help you arrive at impact in a position to see the back of the ball, enabling you to drive a nail through it with your clubhead. TOUR players are extremely talented and coordinated individuals and feel they are turning their hips toward the ball, but they also have some lateral movement as well.

DOWNSWING

Speed is increasing as centrifugal force whirls the clubhead around the extended swing arc. As you return inside the ropes for a close-up look at our professionals' downswings, their shaft positions may seem strange for a so-called extended swing arc. The shaft is almost straight up and down and does not appear to be moving quickly.

The entire downswing, from the top of the backswing to the follow-through, takes only a half-second of elapsed time. The photos were shot between $\frac{1}{4,000}$ to $\frac{1}{8,000}$ of a second to freeze the action. The clubheads are moving very quickly, and the swing arc looks much wider as the shaft becomes parallel to the ground.

In this section, Scott McCarron demonstrates the role that smaller body movements have on building the centrifugal force through the swing arc.

On the Practice Tee, Martin Hall continues his transition drill to get you into the correct position for impact.

Time to look at—and learn from—some great downswings.

Downswing: John Daly

This where the "rip it" expression from my book, *Grip it and Rip It*, comes in. My weight is transferring toward the target as I pull the almost-vertical shaft down with my extended left arm. The shoulders are unwinding, and the clubhead is moving smoothly but quickly building velocity.

The smaller photo below shows how the pull of centrifugal force is beginning to extend the shaft out and away from my body as the downswing continues.

My right shoulder is now lower than my left, as it was at address.

My extended left arm, unwinding shoulders, weight transfer, and the pulling-down motion with my left hand, combine to rapidly build clubhead speed.

Look at the large muscles of my lower body—the thighs. Is there any doubt where the power is coming from? My leg drive is evident, and the firm lower base is providing the balance for a smooth weight transfer.

With my thumb and trigger finger still not closed, my upper body rotation is quickly catching up to my lower body.

As you look at this photo, can you see how my hips have cleared past the ball, leaving room for the rest of my body to sweep the club through?

Steve Pate has been our body-flex specialist, and here's a good example of what he's been telling you. My spine angle has remained constant because of the flex. Long, accurate drives depend on having your body return along the same path it took on the backswing.

My spine angle is exactly as it was when I addressed the ball.

The thumb and trigger finger are still not touching. The grip pressure is on the last three fingers of my left hand.

My hips have turned past the ball, clearing room for the upper body to sweep the club through.

As I transfer my weight toward the target, my right heel begins to rise up. I'm feeling more weight on the ball of my left foot, and the foot will swivel around shortly.

DOWNSWING: JOHN JACOBS

Looking at this photo you might think I'm keeping my weight on the back foot as my shoulder rotation is pulling the club down. However, my left leg is starting to lean toward the target, indicating the weight is in the process of transferring forward.

The bending of the shaft illustrates how much force is being exerted on the clubhead as centrifugal force builds. Left arm extension continues to keep the swing arc wide and the speed of the clubhead increasing and on plane.

You don't need to swing your arms fast. Just make the body movements with a relaxed grip, and the clubhead speed will develop naturally. In the smaller inset photo, you can see centrifugal force pulling the clubhead away from the body as it approaches the ground. My arms are still extended and I'm maintaining my wrist angle.

My right knee begins to tilt toward the target because it no longer needs to support my backswing body weight.

My swing tempo smoothly accelerates on the downswing. Begin your transition with your lower body and then smoothly accelerate as you unwind, reaching your maximum velocity at impact.

My extended left arm transfers the pulling motion efficiently to the shaft. I feel my left side pulling back toward the target.

The left side of my body pulls me back toward the ball. Pulling, or rotating the left hip, is my swing key to transfer the weight back toward the left side. Remember: Weight away from the target on the backswing and toward the target on the downswing. If you finish facing the target and all your weight is on your left side, you'll drive the ball longer and more accurately.

DOWNSWING: SCOTT McCARRON

My balance begins to shift from my right to the left side. As you look at the main photo on this page, notice that I'm staying behind the ball and not allowing my body to pass in front of it. The weight may be going forward but the body stays behind at this point.

The pulling-down motion starts kicking the clubhead speed into high gear, and the inset photo shows the club working away from my body as the backswing continues. Notice the wrists have not released.

The extended arm and transferring my weight toward the target are building centrifugal force on the clubhead. I'm not moving away from the ball to create the effect.

Clubhead speed is created by the smooth, smaller rotational movements of your body. Power is being transmitted through my arm and shaft to the clubhead.

My wrist hinge is intact.

As my weight shifts, my balance is transferring toward the target.

As you look at my swing, understand that while it is happening I am focused only on one objective—getting the ball to the target. I have zero swing thoughts except for that.

Confidence in my swing lets me trust it and just let it go. Cluttering your mind with swing thoughts overloads perhaps the most efficient of all computers, your brain. Focus on your target, let it go and enjoy the game.

Sensing the transfer of weight away from my right side, the right heel begins to rise. The foot will pivot so I can finish my swing facing the target.

Ignite your driving power. John Daly and I demonstrate the Little Circle/Big Circle Drill, and how it is related to smooth body movements, in Chapter 5.

DOWNSWING: STEVE PATE

Ben Hogan, a legendary champion who overcame more serious physical injuries than me, said he defined the downswing as "starting the hips back and then hitting the ball as hard as I can with my upper body, my arms and my hands, in that order."

If you have a friend who swings and then partially follows through still facing the ball or extremely right of the target, that's a golfer who does not clear his hips on the downswing. You can't finish facing the target unless

your hips move out of the way to allow your upper body to swing through.

Driving for distance and accuracy depends on delivering the clubhead to the ball square to the target line. As they unwind back to the ball, your hips need to get out of the way. While your shoulders must be square to your target line at impact (ball flight begins in the direction of the shoulder line at impact), the line of your hips should be slightly open (left) to the target line.

My left arm stays extended as it pulls the club down and my shoulders unwind.

On my downswing, the hips are clearing through the impact area and the unwinding shoulders are quickly catching up.

As you look at two views of my downswing, notice how I work the shaft to a position parallel to the target line as it approaches horizontal. For this shot to draw back into the wind, I want the clubface to approach the ball on a shallow path.

If I stay relaxed and tension free, my right arm will turn over the left past impact, and put a right-to-left spin (draw) on the ball. All this can happen naturally if you begin your downswing smoothly with your legs and hips, and quickly accelerate them toward and through the impact area. Allow your left side to lead the way.

Your flex retains your spine angle. This constant angle allows your two athletic body rotations (back and through) to follow the same line. The clearing of the hips will allow the right side of the body to fire through the impact area, producing a longer and more accurate drive.

PRACTICE TEE

To make sure you swing the club down on a better plane and smack the back of the ball, most members need some lateral motion to start the downswing. This lateral motion lowers your right shoulder, putting you in position to powerfully impact the ball as the clubhead approaches from the inside track.

The best drill I can recommend is actually a continuation of the leftfield hip sliding drill from the previous chapter.

LEFTFIELD HIP TRANSITION DRILL II

As you will recall, I placed a stick behind my right heel toward my left toe, providing a line for the proper distance and direction required for initiating lateral hip movement during the transition. As the hips move laterally, they bring the arms down naturally and start the club accelerating along its proper plane.

While it may appear this lateral movement has kept my weight on the right side, it's shifting toward the target as the left leg shows.

1 This is how you left me in the last chapter as the hips shifted laterally toward leftfield. As a result of the hip movement, the arms were automatically pulled down to this position with the club correctly on plane.

2 Because my hips (instead of the shoulders) began the transition, the rest of my upper body unwinding will deliver the club from the powerful inside track.

3 As the unwinding continues, the club swings powerfully into the back of the ball at impact. Because of my lateral leftfield hip slide, I'm properly positioned to watch the backside of the ball.

IMPACT

Comparing a golf swing to a rocket launch, liftoff occurs at impact. The success of the flight, however, has already been determined by the launching platform (address), the fueling procedure (backswing), ignition (transition) and the release of energy (downswing).

If the timing and swing plane are correct, centrifugal force will smash the squared clubface into the ball, compressing it for a microsecond before the energized ball flies toward the target.

In this section, our four TOUR professionals are shown at impact—the moment when the choreography, coordination and timing of all the body movements come together.

On the Practice Tee, Martin Hall demonstrates two drills to help develop the important feeling of driving a nail through the back of the ball. While our professionals stress weight transfer, Martin prefers to think of it in terms of winding and unwinding, coiling and uncoiling. Choose the mental image that works best for you.

Liftoff has begun.

IMPACT: JOHN DALY

My downswing clubhead speed smoothly accelerates and reaches 140 mph at impact. Because I retain my spine angle and swing plane, I return to the ball with a solid impact position, even with my long backswing.

With my hips rotated past impact zone, my body has room to freely swing the club through to a powerful rendezvous with the ball.

I swing around a steady head. Even though the head has slight lateral movement during the swing, it feels as if it has remained still, which helps maintain the correct spine angle. As the shoulders rotate the club to follow-through, the head will be pulled up naturally.

This solid impact position returns my left arm to the on-line position I created at address. My wrists have not released.

The trigger finger has been forcibly closed onto the grip by centrifugal force at impact, just as I said it would. My left-hand grip pressure is in the last three fingers.

My left foot feels the weight and remains in position to support my body weight as I follow-through.

The weight has shifted just past where impact occurred, and as I begin to enter the follow-through portion of my swing, the weight-free right toe will shortly swivel toward the target.

As you look at this position, compare it to your buddies' swings. Can you see the room I've created to swing the club through? Do they? This is a good illustration of how important it is to clear your hips. Your transition from backswing to downswing must begin with the hips leading the way.

If the shoulders start first, the hips will lag behind and the club will get trapped, making it impossible to have centrifugal force pull the clubhead down the swing plane and make impact at maximum velocity.

As the lines illustrate, the shoulders and hips rotate on two different planes. While the hips are level, the shoulders rotate more up and down to allow the club to stay on plane. The spine angle, set at address, is maintained through impact and only changes as the body wraps around on the follow-through.

My right foot is rising and the toe will swivel toward my target.

IMPACT: JOHN JACOBS

I want to catch the ball on the upswing at impact, to put overspin on it. This helps gain additional yardage from a ball that rolls after landing. As you look at the photo, notice how level my driver is, allowing the 8- or 9-degree face to efficiently impart overspin as it launches the ball on a high trajectory.

I return to impact with a solid position.

My weight has shifted toward the target as I impacted the ball. If centrifugal force is the energy and power behind a powerful swing, proper weight transfer provides the fuel.

I raise both heels at impact, as the inset photo at right shows, putting everything I have into the shot. The weight is mostly on the ball of my left foot at this stage.

My hips have cleared, giving me a lot of space to power the club through. My steady head has helped my swing stay on path, and centrifugal force has swung the clubhead to its full impact extension point and directly at the clubhead's sweetspot. My address position set my feet the correct distance from the ball to assure this would occur.

My spine angle has remained constant and my body is flexed to athletically hit this shot. Senior players can drive the ball a long way by following some basic posture fundamentals:

• At address, bend forward from the waist and push your derriere out.

• Put some flex in your legs and feel relaxed.

• Roll back and forth until the balance is on the balls of your feet.

• Maintain the same spine angle throughout your swing.

My right foot rises up on the toe and will shortly swivel to face my target.

My weight is on the ball of my left foot.

FOLLOW-THROUGH EXTENSION: JOHN DALY

Never think about applying the brakes at any point during your swing, if you want to hit longer drives. Allowing the clubhead to finish around your body will encourage the follow-through extension you see in this photo. I'm keeping my swing arc wide even though I'm past impact.

Legendary baseball sluggers don't bunt for a home run, yet that is the kind of position some members may place themselves in when they slow down their swings. Big baseball hitters finish with a wide extension and allow the momentum of centrifugal force to propel the bat around their body.

In the half-second of time it takes to swing from the top of your backswing to follow-through, any decision to purposely slow down must occur before impact and will put a brake on your swing before the clubhead meets the ball. When you should be accelerating, a signal has gone off to slow down. This does not enhance the concept of the free flowing swing. My suggestion: Continue along a wide swing arc by extending past impact and allow centrifugal force to carry you to a complete follow-through.

As I extend out past impact, my head remains the center of my swing. I'm still looking at the impact area, instead of following the ball. The shoulder rotation will pull my head up naturally.

My extended arms and shoulder line forms a powerful triangle. If you can develop the feeling of staying connected with the club shaft pointing at your chest, you will be able to continue a powerful swing to completion.

My normal flight pattern draws the ball from right to left. Compare my arm and wrist positions with those of Scott McCarron, who fades the ball. My forearm rotates the right hand over the left past impact, where Scott's right hand will be on the side of the club in the same position.

Follow-through extension powerfully to keep the swing arc wide, allowing the momentum of centrifugal force to continue past impact. Never put on the brakes!

Your first impression when analyzing this photo should be how much room I had to power my clubhead through the ball. My hips cleared and the unwinding of my upper body continued without being trapped. The results: maximum clubhead speed at impact; and a swing plane that allowed the clubhead to follow an inside track to the ball, squared to the target line at impact.

My shoulders continue rotating on the more up-and-down oblique line, while my hip rotation is more level.

FOLLOW-THROUGH EXTENSION: JOHN JACOBS

Past impact, I continue my extension and the transfer of weight to the left side. My body continues its turn while my head remains in the impact position. My hips and shoulders are naturally unwinding with the momentum of my golf swing. It may look as if I'm leaning to the right, but the weight has been pulled over to my left side and toward the target.

If you follow the old adage of "keeping your head down," you may be losing distance because of a misconception. Consciously trying to maintain a head down position tends to make you decelerate the club, flipping it through the drive.

Allow the full extension of your follow-through to pull your head up without resistance. When your head rotates up naturally, you'll be able to see your long and accurate drive heading straight at the target.

The triangle of the arms, hands and chest is the mirror image of how they looked at the first part of my takeaway. The full extension of my arms is working the shaft down the line.

I would never be able to raise my right heel unless my weight had transferred over toward the left side. Looks may be deceiving and contribute to many amateur golfers' misunderstanding of proper weight transfer.

ollow-through extension is just as important as every other position in my golf swing. I must extend through impact to drive the ball long and on target.

Golf swings are fluid movements rather than posed positions. To help work on your swing, try and emulate this position to develop a feeling of extending your swing arc through the follow-through.

My shoulders rotate on the same pivot axis I set at address. The right shoulder is correctly working down and through, instead of around and high.

My right forearm is rotating the right hand over the left as I extend down the line. This produces a slight draw. On the next page, Scott McCarron demonstrates a fade (controlled left-to-right ball flight) for comparison.

FOLLOW-THROUGH EXTENSION: SCOTT McCARRON

While this follow-through extension position may look like John Jacobs', notice the difference in our hands. My right hand is on the side of the shaft while his is more on top. I'm fading the ball and he's drawing it.

For a controlled fade, hold back the forearm rotation a little longer before allowing the right hand to come over the left. Maintaining the tri-angle relationship of shoulders, arms and hands is important in order to continue the swing along the arc.

Incorrectly bending the left arm and wrist, a problem for some members, creates a blocking effect on the clubhead. This destroys power and precision by altering the swing plane and degrading the centrifugal force. The ball would start out right and continue weakly off target.

The triangle illustrates my powerful extension through impact. Maintaining a light grip keeps my arms tension-free and allows centrifugal force to extend the arms out as the weight of the clubhead passes through impact at maximum velocity.

My right hand stays more to the side of the club as I fade the ball. A draw would have the right forearm rotating the right hand over the left in this position.

My ball begins its flight toward the tree but will fade to the right around the bunkers. Notice how my arms are working down the slightly open shoulder line I set at address.

Members who start the ball off line to the left and watch as it slices into the right rough may be aiming their shoulders and feet to the left while the clubhead is aimed down or to the right of the fairway. That swing plane slices the face across the ball from an outside-to-in path.

Try this: Have targets to aim at, even on the practice range. Set your feet, knees and shoulders parallel to the target line as you address the ball. Top professionals always work on address, and so should you.

My shoulders are working down and under the ball. I retained my spine angle all the way through this position.

Elements
of the
Swing:
Follow-
Through
Extension

113

FOLLOW-THROUGH EXTENSION: STEVE PATE

I have tremendous respect for the athleticism of many of my pro-am partners. They have to be incredible athletes just to get back to the ball from some of the swings I see. As you look at our swings, simplicity really is the key. Even this follow-through extension happens naturally.

My drive will draw back into the powerful crosswind because I stayed on plane and maintained my power position while extending out during follow-through. Here's my simple approach:

• A light grip keeps the arms and wrists tension-free, allowing me to feel the clubhead.

• Body flexibility maintained the same spine angle on my backswing and on my follow-through extension.

• My wide swing arc that began with the takeaway continues through impact.

• I stay on plane and the ball will begin its flight on my target line before drawing left. My body motions are smooth throughout my swing.

My head remains in the impact position even as my shaft extends out parallel. As my shoulders rotate around, they will bring my head up naturally without any conscious effort on my part.

The weight of the clubhead, powered by centrifugal force, is rotating my right arm, bringing my right hand over my left. The clubface closes to the target line almost immediately after impact, imparting right-to-left spin on the ball and a ball flight that draws.

Analyzing my extended follow-through position from the target looking back illustrates some very key points as to how I executed this shot. Especially look at the room I have to power my body through. Centrifugal force is extending the clubhead out on a wide swing arc.

With a club on the ground to check my alignment, the ball starts out on target before drawing back to the left. If I played a straight shot down the center of the fairway in this crosswind, the ball would be blown into the right rough.

Maintaining the same spine angle set at address is vital to the success of any swing. My body flex, along with a steady head, allowed me to swing back and through with the same fixed spine angle.

The right hand rotates over the left, closing the clubface after impact.

The face is closed and parallel to the target line. The ball will draw back into the wind, landing at my target in the fairway.

PRACTICE TEE

Earlier, I demonstrated some drills that included swinging the club past impact. Many golfers quit on their swings at impact without realizing the clubhead needs to continue along the swing arc.

Any premature braking affects both distance and accuracy. The drills in this section will help train your muscles to allow the clubhead to swing unrestricted through impact all the way to the finish position.

SPLIT GRIP DRILL

This is a swing maintenance drill that golfers of all levels should do regularly. It helps you time both sides of the body. When you swing the club down, the motion requires both a pulling by the left arm and a pushing by the right arm. These forces should be about equal. Splitting the grip helps you develop that feeling.

2 Watch the grip as you take the club back.

1 Hold the club waist high and grip it with your left hand on top and the right hand under the grip.

3 Swing toward the target and feel the balance of pulling and pushing as the arms work together. Your forearm will rotate properly through the impact zone and release the wrists naturally as it extends out.

DAVIS LOVE JR. DRILL

This is a good drill to help you feel the clubhead squared up at impact and closed as it goes through the ball. This drill will also help you keep the left side of your face behind the ball.

You can hit a ball with this drill. I'll show you how to set up for it properly.

1 Begin this drill with a good address position.

2 Raise your left foot on its toes.

3 Rotate back to the top of your backswing while staying in balance. Swing through the ball from this position. This drill will also help you work on swing rhythm as you maintain your balance.

HORIZONTAL SWINGING

You must swing the club in an arc to develop power and accuracy. Swinging the club horizontally reinforces the concept of the swing arc. The whooshing sound develops an awareness of clubhead speed.

1 Swing the club back on a horizontal plane.

2 Smoothly accelerate as you swing the club horizontally toward the target.

3 If you swung the club on a horizontal swing arc, you would have heard a whooshing sound that reached its loudest around impact. Practice swinging at different speeds to find the best swing tempo for you.

FOLLOW-THROUGH FINISH

In this section, our four professionals coast to a finish as they complete their swings facing the target. John Jacobs suggests that some members may want to work on their swings starting from this balanced position, and he provides tips on how to do it.

Scott McCarron leads off the Practice Tee this time, with two drills he uses to help his balance and extension. Swinging in balance will add yards and accuracy to your drives.

Martin Hall demonstrates a Practice Tee drill for members who have a problem with their chin blocking shoulder rotation.

Let's finish our swing the right way. Here's how.

FOLLOW-THROUGH FINISH: JOHN DALY

Centrifugal force has brought the club to the completion of my swing. I never tried to purposely stop the club, but allowed momentum to swing the clubhead around my body.

The only acceptable finish position for driving the ball powerfully and accurately is facing the target. I'm perfectly balanced and comfortable while watching my ball fly far and long toward the target.

The shaft worked its way across my back, indicating I stayed on plane throughout the swing.

I hit against a firm left side, as the line illustrates.

The weight has transferred to my left side, allowing my right foot to pivot; the laces face the target.

My ball is tracking over the desert and will draw to the left, setting up my favorite 85-yard lob wedge approach. I love that shot, and confidence reduces tension and allows the swing to be free and easy.

Part of my pre-shot routine—which I'll show you in Chapter 7—is to visualize the ball in flight and tracking toward the target. Visualizing the ball flying over the desert, with the mountains as a background, is like looking at a work of art.

Elements
of the
Swing:
Follow-
Through
Finish

121

FOLLOW-THROUGH FINISH: JOHN JACOBS

y weight has transferred to my left side. Clubhead speed is important, but clubhead speed plus weight shift is vital if you want longer drives. I play with pro-am partners who can swing the club as fast as I can, but I outdrive them by 100 yards. The difference is they use only their arms, while I use my lower body to shift my weight and generate power.

If you can generate close to 100 mph of clubhead speed, you should be hitting the ball the same distance as me, but more than likely, you don't. The difference is weight shifting. Before you invest in that $500 driver to gain a few extra yards, try perfecting your weight transfer. It's cheaper and more effective.

My right shoulder has wrapped around my head, allowing the club to come to a natural stop. Some instructors teach working your way back from a good finish position. Try this:

• Using a full-length mirror at home, pose yourself in a finish position similar to ours. Be sure you are facing the target, with your weight on the left side.

• Slowly unwind and extend back to the ball.

• Swing slowly back to the finish position.

• Slowly unwind and go past the impact position in reverse.

• Swing back to the same finish position.

• Unwind and reverse back to the ball, extending farther back every time, and then swing back to the finish.

• As the entire swing becomes longer, work on rhythm as you swing back and forth.

With the weight transferred to my left side, my right foot is free to pivot and face the target.

I'm watching my ball as it flies toward the target. My hips, chest and belt buckle are pointed at the target.

Earlier, I told you that I want to put overspin on the ball so it rolls for additional yardage after landing. The experts say that too much overspin will fly the ball too high, but I'm not concerned about how high I'm going to hit it. You shouldn't be either.

When you get to a certain level, say a 5 handicap or less, or you get on the TOUR, then you start playing to the course. Certain holes and conditions call for either high or low trajectory shots. You adapt.

Throughout this book, Steve Pate has been demonstrating in severe wind. In windy conditions, many professionals will widen their stance, but I choose to narrow mine because I don't want to move too much off the ball. I swing a lot easier when the wind is blowing because balance is so critical. You want to make sure you hit the ball solidly, and it's a lot easier to hit it solidly when you take an easier swing.

Elements of the Swing: Follow-Through Finish

FOLLOW-THROUGH FINISH: SCOTT McCARRON

My swing has come to a satisfying end. The ball faded around the bunker, exactly as planned. As you look at this photo, do you see how balanced and comfortable I am? Balance is something I work on every day. In the Practice Tee section following, I will show you how I work on my balance.

My hands are high above my body, as they were at the top of my backswing. The shaft has worked around my back as it completed the swing.

Totally in balance is the best way to describe this finish position. The line shows how I maintained a firm left side to hit against. I stayed behind the ball and allowed the clubhead to whoosh around my extended swing arc, powered by centrifugal force.

I concentrated totally on getting my ball to the target throughout this swing. Too many swing thoughts can destroy a player's game, and that includes a TOUR player. I trust my swing, and once my target has been selected, I don't let any thought get in the way.

Overlooked by many amateurs, but mandatory for all professionals, is the pre-shot routine. Every motion and action before the ball is struck is exactly the same. This creates a feeling of familiarity and helps to quash nervousness or distractions. It focuses my mind on the job at hand: getting the ball to my target. You'll find my pre-shot routine in Chapter 7.

FOLLOW-THROUGH FINISH: STEVE PATE

In spite of the heavy winds, I maintained my balance throughout the swing. The straight line below shows about 85 percent of my weight has transferred toward the target and is now on my left side as I finish. The strong left side really shows up in this photo.

You can create longer and more accurate drives by adhering to some basic fundamentals of good golf:

- A correct grip that enhances your ability to swing the club on plane.

- Good posture to set and maintain the correct spine angle to rotate around.

- Good alignment. We pros work on it all the time, so should you.

- Ball position. Something as simple as this can immediately help your game.

This is a very balanced finish position with a strong left side.

The natural acceleration of my swing carried me through to a well-balanced finish; in this wind, this was vital to keeping the ball in the fairway. Playing a second shot from the short grass is far better than having to create a par saver from the deep rough or from behind a tree.

Scott McCarron discussed the importance of pre-shot routines. I'm going to demonstrate mine in Chapter 7. How important is it? I spent four months before I finally found one that helped.

Elements
of the
Swing:
Follow-
Through
Finish

127

PRACTICE TEE

The need for balance during your golf swing can't be stressed enough. Once you fall out of balance, the flight dynamics are changed, creating a loss of accuracy and clubhead speed. I have two drills to share with you that have helped improve my balance and my extension.

I use a Styrofoam roller, heavy club and weighted balls. I do this drill indoors without shoes so that I can feel the balance on the roller.

Martin Hall finishes up with his Angle-to-Angle drill, to help you get better shoulder rotation.

—SM

SWING BALANCE DRILL

I stand without shoes (barefoot is also good) on the Styrofoam roller (Photos 1 and 2) at address, using a weighted club to develop a feeling for balance. Being shoeless helps me gain the maximum feeling of the shifting weight and balance points. The key is to maintain a wide swing arc, beginning with a wide extension back (Photo 3).

As I continue to the top of my practice backswing (Photos 4 and 5), I concentrate on being very smooth. I swing down through the impact position (Photo 6) and maintain a wide swing arc

extension as I follow-through (Photo 7) all the way to my finish (Photos 8 and 9).

I make about 20 swings, beginning with a slow tempo. It's very good to do it slow because you feel all the positions of the swing and can detect when you start getting out of balance.

Smoothness is the key, since any needless motion or maneuver will cause you to lose balance. Once you can stay in balance, you will see a tremendous gain in yardage.

BALANCE EXTENSION DRILL

My backswing provides the fuel for launching longer drives. Maximum power is stored by beginning the backswing with a good extension away from the ball, and smooth tempo throughout the swing.

By maintaining a wide swing arc during my backswing, the body becomes fully torqued at the top, with a feeling of the weight being 75 percent on the inside of the right leg.

To develop proper backswing width and work on my balance, I stand on the Styrofoam roller and place a large ball between my knees, a two-pound ball between my forearms and hold a four-pound ball in my hands (Photo 1). I swing back (Photo 2) and through (Photo 3), maintaining my balance during my backswing extension and follow-through extension.

ANGLE-TO-ANGLE DRILL

This is a suggestion to help those members who are unable to get significant shoulder rotation. Big shoulders and shorter necks may be the reason; stiffness can also cause it.

If pointing your chin out while you look down at the ball doesn't help prevent your shoulder from being blocked by your chin, try this approach to gain additional backswing length.

1 This is not the address position of choice, but some members may not be able to raise their chin up; even if they do, the shoulders still contact the chin on the backswing.

2 Bend your elbows to help the clubhead swing farther back. Only go back as far as is comfortable. The angle of the shaft and wrist on the backswing needs to match the same angle on the follow-through.

3 Swing through the ball to a follow-through position that mirrors the angle of the shaft and wrists on the backswing. Practice swinging from angle to angle to develop a sense of timing and rhythm. Allow the symmetry of the angles to work for you.

Elements of the Swing: Follow-Through Finish

4 CORRECTING PROBLEMS

I n this chapter, John Daly, Scott McCarron, John Jacobs and Steve Pate will help you become a longer and more accurate driver by addressing many common mistakes, including grip and ball position.

The key to a powerful swing is that it should be a free-flowing movement. A poor grip or an inflexible address position will not allow your swing to be free flowing; as a result of compensations you make, your distance and accuracy will suffer.

Partners Club member Richard Spickerman of Orlando, FL demonstrates some of the more common faults. Since joining the club, Richard has lowered his handicap from 22 to 11.

TEE BOX

Even if you don't want to immediately change your game, here are some quick tips that will help keep your ball in the fairway. Just knowing on which side of the box to tee the ball can work to your advantage.

A SLICER'S MISTAKE

Richard has teed his ball in the center of the tee box. His club is aimed down the center of the fairway but his foot and shoulder positions are open. A slice that ends up in the right rough is inevitable.

If you slice or hook the ball, you can drive more balls in the fairway just by choosing the correct spot to tee from. See John's Tip for the Tee, below. As you improve, adjust the position for the shape of the drive you plan to hit.

JOHN'S TIP FOR THE TEE

I teed four balls to show how tee box placement can keep your ball in the fairway. A left-to-right slicer should choose position No. 1 and aim the club to the extreme left side of the fairway. Teeing on the far right side provides double the amount of fairway with which to work. The ball will start left and slice back to the center or right portion of the fairway. Position No. 2 is for a controlled fade.

I plan on hitting a slight draw, so I've chosen position No. 3. If you hit a big hook, then use position No. 4 and aim to the far right side of the fairway and let your ball hook back into play. —*JD*

| #4 Serious Hook | #3 Controlled Draw | #2 Controlled Fade | #1 Slicer |

GRIP

Becoming long and accurate off the tee begins by examining your grip. It may feel comfortable to you, but will it help or hinder your improvement?

INCORRECT GRIP

The incorrect grip Richard is demonstrating is a common mistake. With the right hand under the grip, as evidenced by the V pointed outside his right shoulder, he will encounter great difficulty attempting to make a power producing, free-flowing swing that stays on plane.

SCOTT'S CORRECT GRIP

I want the V's of both hands pointed just to the inside of my right shoulder. The club should also be held in the fingers, but because of my small hands, I grip it slightly more in the palms than do most long drivers.

Grip the club lightly. A grip that is too tight creates tension in your wrists and forearms, preventing a free flowing swing. A good "feel key" is to relax your grip to the point where you can sense the weight of your driver head at the top of your backswing.

—SM

POSTURE

A powerful golf swing requires two athletic rotational movements—one on the backswing and the other on the downswing. Adapting an athletic posture at address enhances your ability to hit longer and more accurate drives consistently.

INCORRECT POSTURE

This is not the address position you want for increasing power and precision off the tee. Standing straight with locked arms is as bad as slouching over the ball. The absence of body flex at address destroys any chance of achieving consistent length and accuracy.

STEVE'S CORRECT POSTURE

This position allows me to make a consistent rotation back and through the ball. If you substituted a football for my golf club, you would see the position is similar to how a quarterback looks when taking a snap.

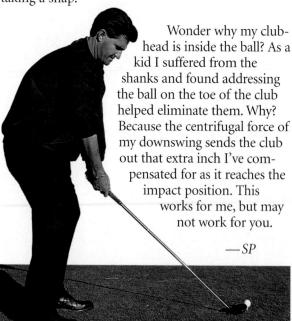

Wonder why my clubhead is inside the ball? As a kid I suffered from the shanks and found addressing the ball on the toe of the club helped eliminate them. Why? Because the centrifugal force of my downswing sends the club out that extra inch I've compensated for as it reaches the impact position. This works for me, but may not work for you.

—SP

BALL POSITION

Accurate drivers deliver the clubface square to the target line at impact. This occurs naturally if the swing plane brings the driver from the inside as it approaches the ball, squares at impact, and then continues back to the inside on the follow through.

Impact should occur at the bottom of the downswing arc. The bottom of the swing arc for the driver is toward the front of your stance.

TOO FORWARD

You will never maximize your potential length or have consistent accuracy by teeing the ball this far forward. It is a Band-Aid compensation for other swing problems. The usual result from this position is either a pull to the left, if the clubface is closing at impact; or a slice to the right as the open clubface cuts across the ball, applying left-to-right spin.

TOO FAR BACK

Depending on your swing plane, this ball position will either produce a big hook or a drive that immediately goes right. Sometimes a wind shot requires adjusting the ball back in your stance, but never this far.

SCOTT'S POWER BALL POSITION

My ball is correctly positioned off my left heel. In this power position, a straight line can be drawn down my left arm through the shaft. Compare the line with those in Richard's incorrect ball positions. At address, I want my arm and club pre-set to the same position they will be in when impacting the ball. —SM

JOHN'S POWER BALL POSITION

The straight line can also be drawn down my left arm through the shaft. Richard's incorrect ball positions set his arms and shaft at an angle. A powerful golf swing is also a simple golf swing. The fewer moving parts the better. Richard's arm/shaft angle is sure to cause a breakdown because it won't allow him to be solid coming back to the ball. —JD

WEIGHT TRANSFER

Many TOUR professionals agree the No. 1 problem for the amateur golfer is understanding where the body's weight should go to create a powerful golf swing. Martin Hall provides some help in our drill section, but John Jacobs illustrates weight shifting here to help you visually understand it.

REVERSE WEIGHT PIVOT

Richard can't help smiling as he demonstrates a version of the reverse pivot, seen every weekend on golf courses around the world. He used to be a *reverse pivoter*, but never realized it. His body weight is incorrectly on his front leg on the backswing and transferred over to his back leg on the downswing. This is the reverse of what you want to achieve.

JOHN JACOBS' POWER WEIGHT TRANSFER

My 284-yard drives are a result of transferring the weight of my body correctly:

Backswing—The weight has been transferred over my right side as the firm right leg and bent left leg show.

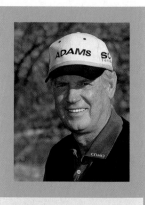

Impact—The weight is correctly transferring over to my left side as the raised right heel proves. My head has stayed behind the ball but my weight is going forward.

Follow-through—All my weight has transferred to my left side.

—JJ

JOHN SAYS:

Try This Practice Tip:

1 Swing to the top of your backswing and attempt to raise your left foot. If the weight has transferred back, you can raise it; if not, you reverse pivoted.

2 Swing to your follow-through position and attempt to raise your right leg. If the weight has correctly transferred forward, you can raise it; if not, you reverse pivoted.

SHOULDER ROTATION

The farther you can take the club back, the more clubhead speed you will generate on the downswing. Ideally, you should be able to rotate your left shoulder under your chin on the backswing. Sometimes the chin blocks the shoulder, limiting the backswing rotation.

BLOCKED SHOULDER

There may be two reasons why Richard's chin has blocked his shoulder. Sometimes golfers tuck their chins into their chests as they address the ball. As the left shoulder rotates back, the chin blocks it and the backswing either ends or is bumped off plane.

Golfers who have shorter necks and wider chests may also have this problem. John Jacobs offers a couple solutions here, and Martin Hall suggests an angle to angle approach in the drill section.

JOHN'S CHIN UP ADDRESS

You can still see the ball at address with your chin up. It is important to set up with enough space for your left shoulder to rotate under your chin as the driver reaches the top of your backswing.

—JJ

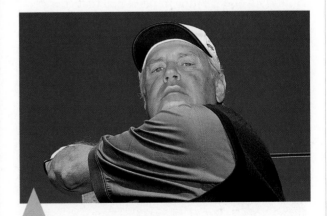

LEFT SHOULDER UNDER CHIN

With my chin up, I have room for my left shoulder to fit under my chin. This is a very simple solution to a very common mistake many golfers make at address.

—JJ

Correcting Problems

DOWNSWING

Make a correct backswing and you are almost assured of making a good downswing, if you understand how to begin the transition. The body should be fully wound up and ready to release all the stored energy. The key is to begin the acceleration back to the ball from the ground up. Let your lower body lead the way.

OVER-THE-TOP RELEASE

Richard incorrectly began his downswing from the top instead of the ground, meaning his arms began the downswing instead of his lower body. The clubhead will be impacting the ball from outside the target line instead of taking the power-producing inside track.

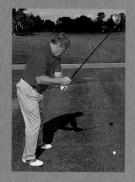

STEVE'S HIPS LEAD THE WAY

This is the top of my backswing. I have fully wound up and it's time to release all that energy back to the ball.

Compare this photo to my backswing photo, below left. See how my hips have rotated back to the ball, leading the way. My arms have reached the parallel-to-the-ground position and the club is still on an inside plane that will deliver it to the ball at maximum acceleration.

Richard's over-the-top release destroys the positive role centrifugal force plays in the swing. The arms alone can never generate the clubhead speed that a lower body transition can.

The driver impacts the ball with maximum clubhead speed. Once you improve your backswing, be sure and master a lower body transition to take advantage of all the energy you stored up as you reached the top.

—SP

FOLLOW-THROUGH

As the released energy rockets the club through the ball at impact, allow that energy to come to a natural stop in a complete follow-through position. Maximum power will be diminished if you apply the brakes.

INCOMPLETE FOLLOW-THROUGH

Richard stopped the club instead of allowing it to continue to a natural finish. When you apply the brakes too early, the clubhead actually begins slowing down prior to impact. Richard should be facing the target at the finish of his swing.

JOHN FACES HIS TARGET

One good turn deserves another. As you can see, my back faces the target on the backswing (top photo) and my chest faces the target when I follow through. This allows me to attain a high clubhead speed and drives of more than 300 yards.   —JD

Correcting Problems

5 DEVELOPING DISTANCE AND ACCURACY

I n this chapter our PGA TOUR professionals provide more insights, tips and strategies to help you on your quest toward longer distance and better accuracy off the tee.

Scott McCarron's simple demonstration with his keys will show you how to harness the energy of centrifugal force to power your golf swing. John Daly invites you inside the ropes to look at his swing *without* a club to better understand the role the body plays in generating clubhead speed.

John Jacobs shows you some secrets to proper body alignment, which will increase your accuracy. And Steve Pate gets in the act too, showing you how he lines up to his target.

Let's go build some power and precision into our drives.

DEVELOPING DISTANCE

To hit a ball farther, you need to increase clubhead speed. You can accomplish that by allowing centrifugal force to take over. A visual way to understand how centrifugal force works is for Scott McCarron to demonstrate the "Little Circle/Big Circle" concept. To help your understanding, think of Scott's wrist as your body and the keys as the clubhead of your driver.

LITTLE CIRCLE/BIG CIRCLE

I'm attaching my keys to the end of a rope.

As I move my wrist in a small circular motion, I'm creating a force that is transmitted through the string to the keys. The keys at the end of the string are moving faster than my wrist because the distance they can travel is extended due to the length of the string.

The little circle, my wrist, moves slower than the big circle, the keys.

Centrifugal force will be maintained as long as my wrist movements are circular and smooth. If I make any jerky wrist movements, centrifugal force will be degraded and the keys will no longer be whirling around the circle in the same plane. They might even come crashing down. Falling off plane drastically reduces their circular speed and the direction they were travelling. The same principles apply to your swing, as John Daly shows. —*SM*

CLUBHEAD CENTRIFUGAL FORCE

Scott's smooth circular wrist movements created the centrifugal force necessary to keep his keys moving along their larger arc. Golfers can accomplish the same thing by having a smooth body movement transferring the force out through their arms and club shaft to the clubhead. The key is not only to extend the swing arc out as far as possible so the clubhead has a greater distance to travel, but to also stay on the same plane so the speed can increase. Simply put, your body makes the small circle and your clubhead makes the big circle.

Looking at the smaller motions of my swing without a club helps illustrate the *Little Circle/Big Circle* concept. My body's rotational movement creates the centrifugal force, not my arms. The tempo of this rotational movement is slower than the speed my clubhead will travel.

The backswing extends the width of the swing arc for the club to follow on the downswing.

In the photos that follow, take the opportunity to look at my clubless swing to concentrate on my simple body motions; they are the real source of my power.

1 At address I want the ball positioned at the bottom of my swing arc.

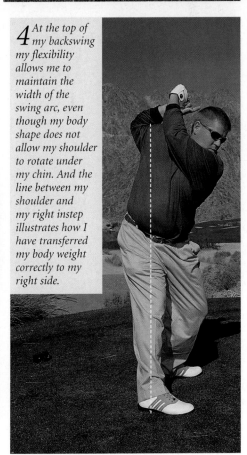

2 As I take the club away, my hands, arms and shoulders move away together. This is a one-piece takeaway.

3 See how my arms extend to create a wide swing arc width as my left shoulder begins to rotate by my chin.

4 At the top of my backswing my flexibility allows me to maintain the width of the swing arc, even though my body shape does not allow my shoulder to rotate under my chin. And the line between my shoulder and my right instep illustrates how I have transferred my body weight correctly to my right side.

I did not rush or jerk my body during the backswing and downswing rotations. Instead, it's a smooth movement following my own unique tempo. While I'm not suggesting that you try to go way beyond parallel on your backswing as I do, try to extend the backswing as far as you can.

5 *My left hip moves back toward the ball and pulling with my left hand initiates downswing. My extended left arm keeps the swing arc wide and centrifugal force working as I stay on plane.*

6 *Approaching impact, the left arm stays extended.*

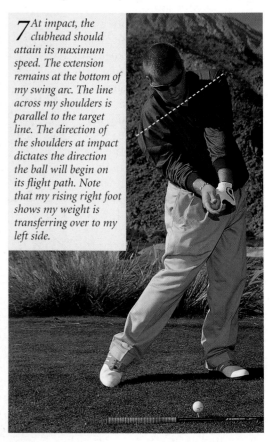

7 *At impact, the clubhead should attain its maximum speed. The extension remains at the bottom of my swing arc. The line across my shoulders is parallel to the target line. The direction of the shoulders at impact dictates the direction the ball will begin on its flight path. Note that my rising right foot shows my weight is transferring over to my left side.*

8 *My arms are still extended, keeping the swing arc wide even after impact.*

9 *For follow-through, the line and raised right foot shows my weight has fully transferred over to my left side. Making a complete follow-through will allow the centrifugal force to bring the club to a natural stop. Note that I finish facing the target.*

A golf swing has many timing elements that will occur naturally if you do not rush your body rotation, and provide a long-enough backswing. I suggest checking your swing without a club in your mirror at home and work on achieving the positions you see in our swings. Find a tempo that is natural to you and practice without a club to develop that feeling.

—JD

DIFFERENT SWING PLANES (SWING ARCS)

Extending the swing arc is essential to all golfers wishing to develop more clubhead speed and additional distance off the tee. The path swing arcs follow (swing planes) may differ between golfers. Jim Furyk is an obvious example with his looping swing, but the usual reason has more to do with height.

At 6-foot-3, John Jacobs (left) has a steeper swing plane than 5-foot-10 Scott McCarron (above). Taller golfers normally have a more upright or steeper swing plane than shorter golfers.

DEVELOPING ACCURACY

Being long off the tee *is* compatible with accuracy. Many of the principles that contribute to longer drives also play a role in having the ball fly on an intended path to the target.

A TOUR player's survival depends on being accurate. On the PGA TOUR, birdie is the name of the game, and consistently reaching a target off the tee is imperative to setting up approach shots. Long drives allow pros to then hit with higher lofted clubs onto greens. Here John Jacobs, Steve Pate and Scott McCarron share some ideas on how you can improve your accuracy and enjoy the best of both worlds— playing short irons off short fairway grass.

BODY ALIGNMENT

DRIVING SECRETS

The driving distance leaders on TOUR are seldom among the leaders in driving accuracy. That's because their length often carries their balls into sloping areas of the fairway, where they can run into the rough. A ball that rolls into the first cut of rough, although very playable, is still a missed fairway.

Place a club on the ground parallel to your target line.

1 Bring your toes to the club.

2 Hold another club up to your chest. Your shoulders should also be pointing parallel to the target line.

3 If the club points left, your shoulders are open, which contributes to your slice.

Driving with water on one side of the fairway requires accurate alignment. While I can work the ball to avoid the water, I still need to be properly aligned to execute the shot.

• I want to align my body parallel to a target line.

• I also want to be sure that my shoulders are parallel to that line.

Some golfers get frustrated because they don't understand why they slice the ball when their feet are parallel to the target line. The reason is their shoulders are inadvertently pointing left of the target. This open shoulder position encourages a slice. Here is a tip to help check your alignment.

—*JJ*

HOW STEVE LINES UP TO THE TARGET

On TOUR we are always laying clubs down on the practice range to check alignment. Even at this level the simplest of things can cause a swing compensation that affects length and accuracy.

Always have a target to aim at when you are on the course or practicing on the range. Here are two tips for working on your alignment.
— SP

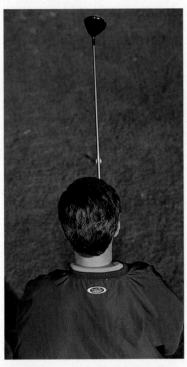

As I stand behind my ball selecting a target, I hold the shaft in front of me. Once I have the target, I bisect the ball with the shaft and find an aiming point on the ground in front of me, along that line, to help align myself.

When I hit a driver, chances are I'll be working the ball with a fade or a draw. My alignment is to the target line I want the ball to start out on. To check my alignment, I practice with a club just inside the ball, aimed along that line, and another club at my feet.

SCOTT PLAYS HIS NORMAL SHOT

If you can learn to hit the ball farther, you can also learn to hit it more accurately. The shape of my normal shot is a fade (a controlled movement from left to right), which is unusual for a long hitter.

To produce the shot, I like to set up a little open, with my shoulders pointed slightly left, and swing down the shoulder line. I constantly work on my basics—grip, alignment and ball position—but aiming left is my tendency. I aim five to 10 yards left of my target and let it fade back.
— SM

I like to check a yardage book to pick out my target. Knowing the distance to carry hazards, or to a downslope, which can increase the roll, is helpful.

During pro-ams I help my amateur partners with their foot alignment the same way I check mine. I put the target line club at my heels instead of my toes.

When I check my alignment, I have someone hold a club along my shoulders. I want my shoulders to point slightly left so I'm properly aligned to hit a left to right fade. I swing along my shoulder line.

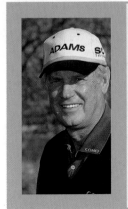

JOHN SAYS:

Earlier, I demonstrated how to make sure your shoulders were parallel to your target line to avoid slicing. The difference between Scott's controlled fade and someone who slices because of poor shoulder alignment is that Scott swings along the line of his shoulders, not the target line.

Developing Distance and Accuracy

147

6

GAME IMPROVEMENT EQUIPMENT

If John Daly or John Jacobs invited you to hit their drivers, you would probably be disappointed with the results. Their equipment matches *their* game, not yours.

Their grip widths, face angles, shaft stiffness and flex points all were carefully evaluated to enhance the accuracy and length of their drives. If golf's top drivers pay close attention to their equipment needs, amateur golfers need to do the same.

In this chapter, Mickey Novack—clubfitter and consultant at David Leadbetter's Golf Academy in Orlando, FL—provides helpful information on heads, grips and shafts. These ideas can play a significant role in increasing your driving power and precision.

QUICK FIX: LOFT SELECTION

Do you have difficulty getting your ball airborne for any appreciable distance? Most likely your swing is bringing the driver face on a downward approach to the ball, causing a 9-degree driver face, for example, to close down to about 6 degrees.

If you are not ready to make swing changes, you can immediately improve your air time by switching to a driver with 12 to 13 degrees of loft. Now your downward approach will de-loft the club to 9 degrees at impact.

When your problem is that you sky the ball off the tee, causing a loss of valuable distance, select a less lofted club with a 7- or 8-degree clubface. Your skied shots are caused by swinging up on the ball. A less lofted club will provide less loft at impact, lowering your launch angle; you should immediately gain more distance.

A driver with 12 degrees of loft (left) will launch your ball higher than an 8-degree clubface (right). All else being equal, you can alter your ball's "sky time" by the club you choose.

LEAD TAPE

Lead tape, available at pro shops and specialty stores, can be applied to the back or side of your driver. Tape applied low on the back will help the ball fly higher by lowering the center of gravity.

If you want to encourage a draw, the tape should be placed on the right side of the driver; the left side for a fade. However, lead tape can only provide a slight difference in ball flight and is not a cure for slicing or hooking.

Arnold Palmer's range bag reflects his love of tinkering with and testing his clubs. He puts lead tape on the back/right of his drivers to encourage a draw; the lead tape adds slightly more swingweight to the clubhead's outside edge.

7 TOUR TECHNIQUES

Flexibility enhances good technique, and in this chapter Nick Price demonstrates golf cart stretches, supervised by rotational flexibility specialist Chris "Mr. Stretch" Verna. Chris originated and developed the "Healthy Stretching" system to prevent golf injuries and to increase performance levels.

Consistency is the hallmark of good golf. For TOUR players, it begins with consistent pre-shot routines. Scott McCarron, John Daly and Steve Pate share their thoughts on the subject in hopes it will inspire you to develop a pre-shot routine that helps your game. John Jacobs and Steve provide TOUR technique applications for working the ball.

On the Practice Tee, Martin Hall concludes the chapter and the book with additional instruction to help you develop a draw or a fade from the ground up. If you slice or hook the ball, learning how to work it in both directions can help shed your current habit.

Let's complete the last leg of our journey to longer, more accurate drives.

CALF STRETCH

Nick stretches his calves, which are the muscles below the knee. The key to this drill is to have the knees straight, the hips over the ankles and the shoulders over the hips. Slowly do this stretch three times, holding in the down position for 15 seconds.

1 Stand on the floor of the golf cart with your hands holding onto the roof. The balls of your feet should be on the edge of the floor with your heels extending out past the edge.

2 Lower your heels gently as you feel the stretch in the back of your lower legs. Hold for 15 seconds and repeat twice.

LONG DRIVER SHOULDER TURN STRETCH

Loosen up your big shoulder muscles with this stretch. Working together with the large muscles of the legs, a powerful force can be unleashed, propelling your ball well beyond your normal landing area.

There are two stretch positions, so hold each one for 15 seconds, then alternate shoulders by changing your golf cart position. All these healthy stretches provide maximum benefit by doing them slowly and gently.

1 Nick begins this stretch in a good athletic position, sideways to the cart, before bending forward. He reached across and grabbed the seat armrest with his lower hand while placing his top hand toward the top of the seat.

2 Nick stretches to the first position by gently pushing the top hand while pulling the lower hand. Observe how his shoulder has rotated more under his chin. Hold for 15 seconds.

3 To stretch to the second position, Nick releases his top hand from the seat, slowly rotating it to a vertical position. Only stretch as far as you can go comfortably, and never force your body into a position. Hold for 15 seconds and reverse shoulders. Always reverse shoulders between stretches and repeat for a total of three times.

WRIST FLEXIBILITY STRETCH

Flexible wrists are important to the success of your golf swing. It's also important to stretch the wrists in two directions to assure overall flexibility. Do each side three times, holding for 15 seconds.

1 Nick bends forward and places the backs of his hands on the cart seat. He gently leans forward as he stretches the wrists. Hold 15 seconds.

2 For the second wrist stretch, Nick places his palms on the seat so his fingers face toward him or just off to the side. Hold for 15 seconds and repeat both positions for 15 seconds.

UPPER BODY STRETCH

Begin this healthy stretch by pre-setting the arms at the extension position. As the head slowly rotates away from the cart, the neck, shoulders and abdomen feel the torque building up for a very gentle stretch. Change positions, and stretch each side of your upper body three times.

1 Nick stands sideways to the cart and reaches his outside arm across his chest, holding onto the roof.

2 With his arm in the extension position, Nick slowly rotates his head away from the cart and holds for 15 seconds. Stretch the other side of your upper body by changing the direction you were facing and reach across your chest, grabbing the roof with your other hand. Repeat both sides for a total of three times each.

The benefits of stretching before you play are obvious, but Chris suggests repeating the stretches *after* your round too. The number of strokes it took for your round are actually body rotations. Double that number, because your body has to rotate both ways to strike the ball, and that's excluding the practice swings as well as the bending to tee your ball or to take it out of the hole.

All this rotation has fatigued and shortened your muscles. Taking a few moments will stretch them back to their normal range. You'll feel a lot better and avoid some stiffness later.

If you have some favorite stretches, like putting a club behind your back and turning, or swinging a few clubs together, add those. You want to be relaxed and loose when you get to the first tee.

Tour
Techniques

LOOSEN UP YOUR SWING

Carrying a heavy club in my bag reminds me to warm up before I play or practice. I stretch like Nick, but the club helps develop positive swing feelings while also loosening me up.

I'm sure that teeing up on the first hole is a nightmare for some members. Warming up while feeling power in your swing builds the confidence to make the first drive of the day more rewarding. See a good warm-up technique below.

Injury prevention is another consideration. NASCAR star Dale Jarrett, a pretty good golfer himself, would never begin a race without warming up his tires, and no professional golfer would ever head out to the range without warming up his muscles. In both cases, injuries can occur if proper warm-up procedures aren't followed. TOUR technique requires a flexible, warmed-up body before proceeding to the practice range and the first tee.

—JJ

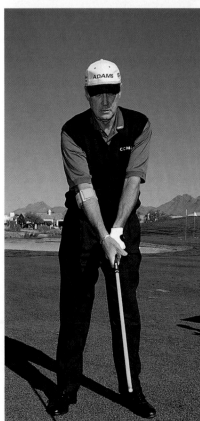

A good warm-up—swinging a heavy club from a good address position to the top of your backswing, down through the impact zone and all the way to a complete finish—sends a message to your muscles that the fun is about to begin.

PRE-SHOT ROUTINES

Long and accurate drives *are* compatible. Incorporating specific target selection into your pre-shot routine—and then setting yourself up properly to that target—improves both accuracy and length.

Golf is a target sport, and our four professionals always have a specific target in mind when addressing the ball. Most amateurs, however, see the wide fairway ahead instead of a precise target such as a pin placement. Consequently, they pay very little attention to aiming at a specific target. John Jacobs informed us earlier that his target selection is based upon pin placement. With a right pin, he prefers a landing spot on the left side of the fairway, and vice versa for a left pin placement.

The location of your drive, even on the fairway, plays a role in ultimately making a birdie, par or bogey. Scott McCarron and Steve Pate have incorporated target selection thoughts or aids into their pre-shot routines.

THE SMALLER THE TARGET THE BETTER

Earlier I told you that once I address the ball, my only swing thought is getting the ball to the target. I want to visualize it flying on the line I choose. My visualization begins even before I tee the ball.

Once the driver is pulled, I stand behind the tee trying to determine which side of the fairway I want to be on. I pick a spot where I want the ball to start out, where I want it to land and where I want it to roll. Very specific targets work best and the smaller the target the better. Here's what I look for:

- I look for fairway mowing lines as potential aiming points.

- A cloud in the sky or even a corner of it that's in line with my target.

- A tree, especially on a cloudless day.
  —SM

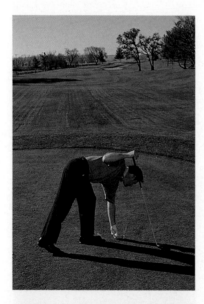

Once my aiming and landing targets are selected, I tee the ball on the side of the box that will help me the most with that particular shot. Here I tee the ball a little right of center for the fade I want to hit.

With my target in mind and visualizing the ball reaching it, I step in and address the ball. Then I just trust my swing.

THREE LOOKS, THREE WAGGLES AND GO!

My pre-shot routine is always the same. I'm very fast and can see the shot I want to hit very quickly, even though I may not execute it perfectly every time. For instance, if I want to hit a 10-yard fade, I visualize my target down the fairway and just carve it there.

For every drive there is a certain side of the fairway I want to be on, and that's my target. Then it's three looks, three waggles and go! When I first came out on TOUR, I used to do two looks and two waggles, but I realized I needed to slow down a little, so I increased it to three each.

—JD

1A *Look at the target.* *1B* *Waggle.*

2A *Look at the target.* *2B* *Waggle.*

3A *Look at the target.* *3B* *Waggle.*

John's pre-shot routine starts with a quick evaluation of where he wants the ball to go.

After three looks and three waggles, the shot is off!

STEVE'S PRE-SHOT ROUTINE

All golfers should have pre-shot routines. Good scores are a result of consistent play, so a consistent pre-shot routine makes a lot of sense. Use our ideas and routines as a starting point, but find something that works for you. Go through the pre-shot routine every time you hit a ball on the course and on the range. It doesn't matter if you waggle three times or two, as long as you do it the same way every time and it works.

Pre-shot routines are like bringing a comfortable room at home to the course. You feel at ease, relaxed and confident in the room, and that's the feeling you need to establish before addressing the ball. Pre-shot routines should also incorporate feelings you need in your swing as well as target selection aids.

—SP

1 Planning the shot.

2 I always begin by standing behind the ball, determining the type and shape of the shot I want to hit. Next, I take a couple of practice swings to develop the necessary feeling to execute it.

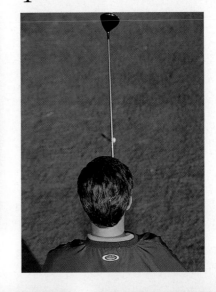

3 Once I have my line where I want the ball to start out, I raise my club, point down that line and bisect the ball. I'm looking for an aiming point, such as a leaf or a long piece of grass that's close to the ball, to align myself to.

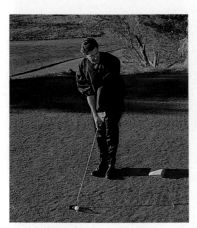

4 Upon stepping in, I immediately set my club on the target line, using the aiming point. A close point is easier to align yourself to than a distant one. If the clubface is properly aimed, I have a better chance of correctly aiming my body along the target line.

5 I set my feet parallel to the target line, widen my stance and adjust my balance into the athletic position we discussed earlier.

6 I spent four months working on the pre-shot routine I'm demonstrating. The two waggles that come next are my own specific choice after trying several alternatives. This routine makes me feel comfortable, because for those four months I went through it every time I hit a ball on the course or on the practice range. It's a trusted part of my game.

THE ACCURACY POWER TRACK

The clubhead is on the accuracy power track as it whirls around and down the swing plane, approaching the ball from inside the target line in order to square up at impact. Impact occurs at the head's sweet spot for this basic approach to long and accurate driving. Working the ball in different directions is a necessity for TOUR players and any golfer wishing to lower his or her score, as John Jacobs and Steve Pate explain next.

Think of your swing plane as an accuracy power track, guiding your clubhead from inside the target line and then squaring up, at impact, at the head's sweet spot.

WORKING THE BALL

TOUR players rarely hit a straight shot. They are usually trying to work the ball to the left or right to reach specific targets. Weather, topography, hazards and pin placement all play major roles in determining if a player plays a left-to-right fade or right-to-left draw and how much of each.

We've seen Scott McCarron fade his ball around a bunker, and Steve Pate draw his ball back into the fairway from the right side. Here John Jacobs and Steve provide more information on how they hit fades and draws, and Martin Hall shares additional techniques on the Practice Tee.

FADE

When I'm fading the ball, I want to feel that the heel of the club is leading the toe through the shot.

FOR A FADE, DELAY THE RIGHT-OVER-LEFT ARM ROTATION

When Steve and I hit fades, we want to hold the right hand from coming over the left as we follow-through. Steve has a short pole in his grip to help you see how the shaft is pointing outside his body in this stage of the follow-through.

This lack of forearm rotation delays the clubface from closing and puts a slight left-to-right spin on the ball at impact, resulting in a controlled fade.

Fades will not release and roll as much as a draw, but they are perfect for situations that require precise landing points. Fades also are important to avoid hazards, like water and sand. Sometimes you want to take hazards out of play by working the ball away from them or starting it out far away and knowing the ball can work back into the fairway without approaching the hazard. Below, Steve has some additional points to help you. —JJ

STEVE SAYS:

- Set your bodyline where you want the ball to start.

- For the fade, you want that to be more to the left.

- It's easier to hit a fade from a forward ball position.

- I grew up hitting a draw, so when I hit a fade I have to think about it a little. The best way is to make the same swing, but hold on to the club a little longer. By holding on, I mean I delay the right-over-left arm rotation.

THE DRAW

Compare this extension photo with the one of my fade. Notice how my right forearm has rotated over my left. This puts a right-to-left spin on the ball. Draws release after landing for additional yardage, and are also used to avoid hazards.

—JJ

Notice that the pointer in my shaft during this draw extension is pointing toward my body. In the fade extension, it's pointing outside my body. This shows a natural right-over-left rotation. The closing club-face puts the draw spin on the ball as it sweeps through impact. Here are some additional tips:

- *To hit a draw, set your bodyline to the right of your target.*

- *I hit a draw from a slightly back ball position, which is tougher with a driver because there isn't much loft.*

- *Try teeing the ball higher.*

—SP

DRIVING
Power &
Precision

PRACTICE TEE

There is no slicing on the road to good golf. You can go from slicing to hooking to good golf, or you can go from hooking to good golf, but you can't go from slicing to playing good golf. Every good player hooked the ball at one time before he or she became a great player.

So learning to work the ball can also serve the purpose of converting those members who presently slice into right-to-left players instead. The first thing you need to understand if you want to work the ball is to avoid the following club-head/ball relationships. One causes an out-of-control slice, the other an out-of-control hook.

THE SLICE

The clubface is open and approaches the ball from the outside to the inside. The open face literally slices across the ball, and the result is a ball far from being under control: A horrible slice!

THE HOOK

The clubface is already closed when it impacts the ball. A hook can take many forms, none of which are helpful when you are trying for distance and accuracy. But better to be a hooker than a slicer.

WORKING THE BALL:
TEE HEIGHT

Let's begin with some basics to help you learn to work the ball properly. Even if you presently slice or hook the ball, learning how to work it like a professional will help your improvement. Let's begin from the ground up.

HIGH FOR A DRAW

Tee up the ball high to help achieve a draw.

LOW FOR A FADE

Tee up the ball low to help achieve a fade.

WORKING THE BALL:
FOOT POSITIONS

Which foot you point has a lot to do with the shot you hit. Using the dog leash practice station to help reinforce alignment, place two small sticks perpendicular to the target line and inside each foot.

The sticks are perpendicular to the line, but your feet should never be perpendicular as mine are here. The question is: Do I want to turn the left foot out and have the right foot perpendicular, or turn the right foot out and have the left perpendicular? Or do I want to have them someplace in between? The partial answer is to go one way or the other, but never in between. The rest of the answer is illustrated next.

LEFT FOOT POINTED OUT

A fade is encouraged, but not guaranteed, the more you turn the left foot out while keeping the right perpendicular to the line. Opening the left foot can speed up the turning of the hips past impact, which helps hit a controlled power fade. This is a classic Ben Hogan position.

RIGHT FOOT POINTED OUT

You can produce more of a hook or draw swing by turning the right foot out and keeping the left foot perpendicular.

Golfers who stand like this are more likely to stop their slice because this position deters the left hip from spinning out of the way.

In essence, what we are doing is using the feet to put the brake on the hips. In this case, we're slowing down the hips as a result of the feet, while in the previous photo we were speeding up the hips.

—MH

WORKING THE BALL: HANDS AND CLUBFACE

The destiny of the clubface position through impact is linked directly to the hands. What the back of your left hand does after impact is what the clubface is going to do.

KNUCKLES UP/FADE

As you look at yourself in the mirror when your hands reach the 4 o'clock position, the knuckles of your left hand point to the sky. This may be an easier way to practice and understand what John and Steve meant when they said they "hang onto it a little longer."

If you delay rotating your forearms, the knuckles will be facing the sky. This also helps if you are trying to eliminate your hook. Practice while facing the mirror and gripping the club just above the clubface. Point your knuckles to the sky, or to your ceiling in this case, and check the clubface position. It's similar to Steve's fade shot extension.

CATCH THE RAINDROPS/DRAW

If you want to draw the ball, the right-arm-over-left rotation features the left palm facing up to "catch the raindrops." This is also somewhat like Steve's posed draw extension. If you want to eliminate your slice and develop an additional distance-producing draw, work on developing this post-impact position.

CREATING FADES AND DRAWS

These lists will help you create fades and draws, eliminate slices and hooks, and increase the length and accuracy of your drives.

TO FADE:

- Tee the ball lower.
- Steve Pate and John Jacobs suggest a slightly farther forward ball position.
- Martin Hall suggested having your right foot perpendicular to the target line and the left toe turned out.
- Everyone agrees you should have the knuckles of your left hand facing the sky after impact. Steve and John referred to it as holding on a little longer, meaning they want to delay the right-over-left natural forearm rotation during follow-through extension.

TO DRAW:

- Tee the ball higher.
- John and Steve recommend a ball position that is slightly farther back in your stance.
- Martin suggested having your left foot perpendicular to the target line and the right toe turned out.
- Everyone agrees you should have the palm of your left hand facing the sky after impact. Martin added to "catch the raindrops." Steve and John referred to it as rotating the right forearm over the left naturally during follow-through extension.

GLOSSARY

Address Your body position (posture, alignment, ball position) as you set-up to the ball.

Addressing the Ball Taking a stance and grounding the club (except in a hazard) before taking a swing.

Approach A shot hit to the green.

Away A player who is farthest from the hole. This player plays their ball first.

Apron Slightly higher grassy area surrounding the putting surface. Also referred to as fringe.

Backspin The spin of a golf ball that is the opposite direction of the balls flight.

Ball Mark The damaged, indented area in the ground caused by the ball when it lands on the green.

Ball Marker Something small to mark the position of your ball on the putting green. You should mark your ball to clean it and also allow your playing partners to have an unobstructed line to the hole. Markers can be purchased, and can be attached to your glove, or use a coin or similar object.

Birdie One stroke under the designated par of the hole.

Bogey One stroke over the designated par of a hole.

Bunker Also referred to as a sand trap.

Blade To hit the ball at its center with the bottom edge of your club.

Blocked Shot Hitting a ball on a straight line to the right.

Bump and Run A type of approach shot that lands and then rolls onto the green and toward the hole.

Carry How far a ball flies through the air. If a water hazard is in front of you, you have to figure the carry to be sure you've taken enough club.

Casual Water A temporary water accumulation not intended as a hazard. Consult the published *Rules of Golf* for information on the relief you are entitled to.

Chili-Dip Hitting the ground before contacting the ball. The result: weak, popped up shots also called "fat."

Divot Turf displaced by a player's club when making a swing. Divots must be repaired.

Double Bogey Two strokes over the designated par for a hole.

Draw A shot that curves from right to left for right-handers and the opposite for left-handed golfers.

Drop The act of returning a ball back into play. Consult *The Rules of Golf* for more correct information on circumstances where this occurs.

Eagle Two strokes under the designated par for a hole.

Fade A controlled, slight left-to-right ball flight pattern. Also can be called a cut.

Fairway Closely mowed route of play between tee and green.

Fore A warning cry to any person in the way of play or who may be within the flight of your airborne ball.

Green The putting surface.

Gross Score Total number of strokes taken to complete a designated round.

Ground the Club Touching the surface of the ground with the sole of the club at address.

Handicap A deduction from a player's gross score. Handicaps for players are determined by guidelines published by the USGA.

Halved the Hole The phrase used to describe a hole where identical scores were made.

Honor The right to tee off first, earned by scoring the lowest on the previous hole.

Hook A stroke made by a right-handed player that curves the ball to the left of the target. It's just the opposite for left-handers.

Hot A ball that comes off the clubface without backspin and will go farther than normal as a result. If a lie puts grass between the clubface and ball, the grooves can't grip the ball to develop backspin. Understanding this, a golfer knows their ball will come out "hot" and plans for that.

Lateral Hazard A hazard, (usually water) that is on the side of a fairway or green. Red stakes are used to mark lateral hazards.

Lie Stationary position of the ball. Also it is described as the angle of the shaft in relation to the ground when the club sole rests naturally.

Local Rules Special rules for the course that you are playing.

Loft The amount of angle built into the clubface.

Match Play A format where each hole is a separate contest. The winner is the individual or team who wins more holes than are left to play.

Mulligan A second ball that's hit from the same location. The shot that's tried again. Limited to friendly, noncompetitive rounds.

Net Score Gross score less handicap.

Par The score a good golfer should make on a given hole. Determined by factoring in 2 putts plus the number strokes needed to cover the yardage between the tee and green.

Provisional Ball A second ball hit before a player looks for their first ball which may be out of bounds or lost.

Pull Shot A straight shot in which the flight of the ball is left of the target for right-handers and right of the target for left-handers.

Push Shot A straight shot in which the flight of the ball is right of the target for a right-handed golfer and opposite that for a left-hander.

Rough Areas of longer grass adjacent to the tee, fairway green or hazards.

Shank To hit a shot off the club's hosel.

Slice A stoke made across the ball, creating spin that curves the ball to the right of the intended target for right-handed golfers and to the left of the target for left-handers.

Stance Position of the feet at address.

Stroke Any forward motion of the clubhead made with an intent to strike the ball. The number of strokes taken on each hole are entered for that hole's score.

Stroke Play Competition based on the total number of strokes taken.

Target The spot or area a golfer chooses for the ball to land or roll.

Top To hit the ball above its center.

INDEX